IMAGES
of Motoring

GENERAL
MOTORS
A PHOTOGRAPHIC HISTORY

The grandson of a Civil War–era Michigan governor, General Motors' founder William Crapo Durant (1861–1947) posed for this portrait in the early 1900s. Durant was a born salesman and promoter who joined with Dallas Dort in Flint, Michigan, in 1886 to form the Flint Road Cart Co. (renamed Durant-Dort Carriage Co. in 1895). After accumulating a small fortune building buggies, Durant was persuaded to invest in the infant Buick Motor Co. in 1904. Just four years later, he leveraged the success of Buick into the creation of General Motors, then brought dozens of other vehicle and parts-supply companies into it. When financial reverses forced him from GM management in 1911, he formed Chevrolet, built it up as a competitor to the Model T Ford, and used it to regain control of GM again in 1916. He was forced out of GM for the last time in 1920. (BH.)

IMAGES
of Motoring

GENERAL MOTORS
A PHOTOGRAPHIC HISTORY

Michael W.R. Davis

ARCADIA

Published by Arcadia Publishing,
an imprint of Tempus Publishing, Inc.
2 Cumberland Street
Charleston, SC 29401

Printed in Great Britain.

Library of Congress Catalog Card Number applied for.

For all general information contact Arcadia Publishing at:
Telephone 843-853-2070
Fax 843-853-0044
E-Mail arcadia@charleston.net

For customer service and orders:
Toll-Free 1-888-313-BOOK

Visit us on the internet at http://www.arcadiaimages.com

CONTENTS

Led by Durant-Dort, Flint buggy production grew hugely during the 1890s and early 1900s, when it exceeded 100,000 units annually. Flint called itself "Vehicle Capital of the World," as shown in this pre-1900 picture of a sign over a downtown street. Note that there were no motor vehicles in the photo. The buggy industry also required many of the same components—axles, springs, wheels, bodies—that could be applied to the new motor cars. (K.)

The following is a key to the photo credits and sources in parentheses at the end of each caption:

B	Buick Public Relations
BH	Buick 90th Anniversary Press Kit
C	Cadillac Public Relations
CH	Cadillac History Services
CP	Chevrolet Public Relations
D	Photos by the author, Michael W. R. Davis
DIS	Daytona International Speedway
F	Ford Motor Company Public Affairs
GA	General Motors Media Archives
GW	General Motors Worldwide Communications
K	Kettering University Archives
M	McCann-Erickson Advertising
N	National Automotive History Collection, Detroit Public Library
O	Opel AG Public Relations
OH	Oldsmobile History Center
OP	Oldsmobile Public Relations Centennial Press Kit
PH	Pontiac History Center
P	Pontiac-GMC Public Relations
R	Reuther Library
S	Saturn Public Relations

All GM photos are copyright 1978, 1998 by General Motors Corp. and used with the permission of GM Media Archives. Kettering University Archives photos are courtesy of Kettering/GMI Alumni Foundation, Collection of Industrial History. Ford photos are from the collections of Henry Ford Museum & Greenfield Village and Ford Motor Company. Reuther Library photos are courtesy of Walter P. Reuther Library, Wayne State University.

INTRODUCTION

I have never owned a General Motors product. In our family photo album, however, there are pictures of my older brother and sister holding a baby—me—while perched on the front bumper of a 1927 Buick, the family car when I was born. It was the only GM car my father ever owned.

To top it off, I spent 25 years in public relations for Ford Motor Company where General Motors was the enemy. So what is a Ford guy doing with a book about GM?

There are three interconnected reasons. First, Detroit is really a small town, a one-industry town, the auto industry. We may be work rivals, but we go to church with one another, our children go to school together, we serve on civic committees together, we play golf together, and we are neighbors. Like members of the armed forces, there is fierce rivalry among us, but we also have learned to pull together as an industry. When one of us is hurt, the other also feels some pain, and we share some delight in one another's successes. Everyone around Detroit might not agree, but that is my take after more than 40 years here.

Second, along the way I have advanced from being merely a history major in college to obtaining a master's degree and completing the course work for a doctorate in history. This pictorial history of General Motors will be the fifth non-fiction historical book that I have written, co-authored, edited, or to which I have been a major contributor.

In particular, this book grew from the Local History Conference at Wayne State University in April of 1998. Among the historical exhibits and patron tables was a booth—actually just a place at a long table—for Arcadia Publishing, staffed by Patrick Catel. I was impressed with Arcadia's approach to making picture histories affordable for local history organizations.

Further, I thought it was ironic that, while historical books about Ford are practically a cottage industry, there is nothing substantive in the book marketplace about giant General Motors. Sure there are good books on the Camaro and the Corvette and several "slice of time" kiss-and-tell revelations taking GM to task for alleged sins, but there are no recent histories.

Because of some earlier journalistic assignments, I was aware there was a catalogue of General Motors historical photographs selected and compiled by a long-time acquaintance, Harold C.L. Jackson Jr., retired from GM's Public Relations Staff, for the corporation's 50th anniversary in 1958 and updated for the 75th. Without Hal Jackson's good staff work at GM years ago, this book would not have been possible.

So I proposed this history of General Motors to Arcadia, and they accepted. What I then had to do was augment the existing photos I had collected for other writing projects, round out the historical narrative to suit my own interpretations, and bring it up to date through GM's 91st year.

As a journalist who has covered the automotive industry for more than 45 years, I have known many of the prominent personalities of the industry. I have participated in countless discussions with other journalists and industry figures about Motor City people, products, organizations, events, and trends—and their interpretations. What is history for scholars, largely documents about past events, I helped create or observed firsthand. This book, therefore, is my version of an important piece of automotive history boiled down to what can be told through pictures and their captions.

The observation "one picture is worth a thousand words" is attributed to Confucius, the ancient Chinese philosopher. I hope this book will make it easy for the young to appreciate GM's history by just flipping through the pages and for serious older readers to gain new insight by following the narrative.

Michael W.R. Davis
Royal Oak, Michigan
August 15, 1999

Admiring a new 1939 Buick are Alfred P. Sloan Jr. (1875–1973), left, long-time president (1923–1937) and chairman (1937–1956) of General Motors Corporation and Harlow H. Curtice (1893–1962), president of GM from 1953 to 1958. At the time of this photo, Curtice was the general manager of Buick. While Durant was the founder of General Motors, it was under Sloan's direction that GM grew from a firm that accounted for about 10 percent of U.S. new car sales in 1923 to become the largest producer of cars and trucks in the world. Sloan was head of the Hyatt Roller Bearing Company of Harrison, New Jersey, when Durant brought it into GM through the 1916–1918 acquisition of United Motors Corporation. (GA.)

One

ROOTS

Various "Blue Ribbon" models of buggies and carriages produced by the Durant-Dort Carriage Company are shown in this photograph of a "showroom" under a county or state fair tent, c. 1900. Note how little has changed from then to today's automobile dealership with its banners, labels, and eager sales force. Southeastern Michigan, just before the turn of the 20th century, was a Mecca for producers of railroad cars, marine engines, cast iron stoves, bicycles, and buggies, creating a pool of skilled workers and manufacturing units that readily fed the infant automobile industry. Other favorable factors included the availability of local venture capital from manufacturing, mining, and lumbering operations, as well as excellent rail and water transportation. (K.)

To Ransom E. Olds goes the distinction of selling the first self-propelled vehicle for export. Olds's first "car" was this one-of-a-kind steam-engined wagon that he built experimentally in his father's Lansing, Michigan machine shop. This resulted in an article in the May 21, 1892 issue of *Scientific American* magazine and attracted the eye of the Frances Times Company of London, England, which bought the machine in 1893 and shipped it to a sales branch in Bombay, India. Within a decade, steam- and electric-powered vehicles were soon bypassed by most developers in favor of the more practical internal-combustion engine. (OH.)

This certificate, dated September 7, 1897, granted Ransom E. Olds 1,250 shares—of the 5,000 issued—in the Olds Motor Vehicle Company organized in Lansing, Michigan. It then took four years for Olds to come forth with a vehicle suitable for production in quantity. (OP.)

BIRTHPLACE OF AUTOMOBILE INDUSTRY
IN MICHIGAN

Shop in which first Oldsmobile was built in 1897. Located
on River St., Lansing, Mich. Photographed in 1922

The first Oldsmobile factory, shown here, was located in Lansing. Subsequently, assembly moved to Detroit where the famous "curved dash" model was developed. A fire destroyed that plant in 1901, but the new model was saved, and Olds production moved back to Lansing, where it remained exclusively until 1936. (GA.)

Early on, Olds also set the industry pattern of using agents for domestic and foreign sales, listing representatives in many North American cities and foreign countries, as shown in this 1900 advertisement. According to automotive trade magazines of the time, the Olds Curved Dash was the most popular car in Czarist Russia during the 1903–1905 period. (OP.)

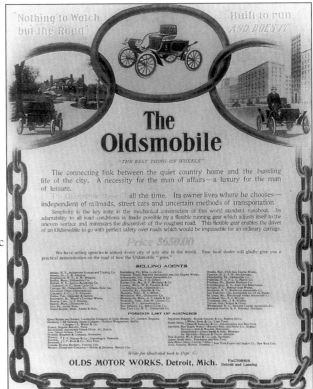

The Olds Curved Dash runabout was the first car to be built on a progressive assembly system. Here, overhead belts and shafts drive the machinery used on the chassis assembly line in 1901. The Curved Dash was the first mass-produced car in America. It had a 60-inch wheelbase, weighed only 650 pounds, and was powered by a one-cylinder, four-horsepower horizontal engine. It was the first car to carry the Olds name and, at $650, sold for $1 per pound. (OP.)

Oldsmobile Curved Dash Advertisement from Early 1900s

Another c. 1901 Oldsmobile advertisement suggested prophetically that the horseless carriage would replace the horse and buggy, a rather presumptuous claim when Olds production was only 425 in 1901, whereas Durant's Flint carriage company was still turning out tens of thousands of buggies annually in the early years of the century. A January 1900 article in *Scientific American* reported an analysis showing it was cheaper to operate a motorcar than a horse and carriage. Olds production reached 2,500 in 1903. (OP.)

In October 1901, Roy Chapin, who would later become head of Hudson Motor Company, drove the Curved Dash from Detroit to the New York Auto Show. The trip took 7 $1/2$ days and 30 gallons of gas. But it was worth it because the trip resulted in approximately 750 orders for new Curved Dashes. (OP.)

Ransom Eli Olds (1864–1950) founded the Olds Motor Vehicle Company on August 21, 1897. He had started tinkering with "horseless carriages" in his father's machine shop in the early 1890s. Like some other early motorcar developers, he did not get along with investors, resigning from Olds in 1904 to start his own Reo Motors, a company which produced automobiles until 1936 and trucks until 1957. "Reo," of course, was Olds's initials spelled out. (OP.)

Henry M. Leland (1843–1932) trained in the arms factories of New England, where precision manufacturing and parts interchangeability had been developed. In 1892, he co-founded Leland & Faulconer machine shop in Detroit, which in a few years became a major supplier to the new auto industry in Michigan. Here, he is shown (left) in his office in 1902, when he had been invited to take over the 1899 Henry Ford Co. after Ford, like Olds, disagreed with investors. Leland renamed the car and company Cadillac and created its quality and reliability image. (N.)

Henry Ford (1863–1947), shown here in his first experimental car, the 1896 quadricycle, actually was the designer of what became the first Cadillac. Many leaders in the automobile industry, including Olds, Chapin, Ford, Chrysler, and Nash, were involved in the early years with what would become General Motors. (F.)

In 1902, the Detroit Automobile Company, established in 1899 and later renamed Henry Ford Co., reorganized as "Cadillac Automobile Company." This 1903 Runabout, Cadillac's first production model, featured a one-cylinder, 10-horsepower engine. The contrast between American cars (mass production) and European cars (limited production) was typified by Cadillac's first-year production of 2,497, versus Vauxhall of England's 43, both in 1903. (CH.)

Here is Ford Motor Company's first car, the 1903 Model A (not to be confused with Ford's 1928–1931 models). Notice the resemblance to the first Cadillac (top), also known as a "Model A." They were both designed by Henry Ford, but the Cadillac had a Leland-designed engine. (F.)

David Dunbar Buick (1854–1929), left, the founder of Buick Motor Co., was a successful Detroit plumbing-fixture manufacturer who turned to making gasoline-powered boat and stationary engines around 1900. He employed two mechanics, Walter L. Marr and Eugene C. Richard, and the three of them developed the valve-in-head automobile engine. W.C. (Billy) Durant, right, invested in Buick in 1904 and quickly used his entrepreneurial skills to make Buick number one in sales, then founded General Motors with Buick profits. Buick production rose rapidly from 37 in 1904 to 4,641 in 1907, when it surpassed Olds and Cadillac combined. (BH.)

The first experimental Buick automobile was built in Detroit between 1898 and 1901 and sold in 1901 to Walter L. Marr (1865–1941), who had probably built it for David Buick. Marr and his wife, Abbie, were photographed here in what is believed to be that first Buick. This print was found in 1993 among the papers of a Marr daughter. Someone had written on the back, "1898" and "first Buick." (BH.)

16

Buick's chief engineer, Walter L. Marr (left), and Thomas D. Buick, the son of founder David Dunbar Buick, were photographed in the first Flint-made Buick as it ended its successful Flint-Detroit round trip in July 1904. (BH.)

The first Flint Buick factory, on West Kearsley Street near the Flint Wagon Works, was originally one story in 1903 and later was expanded to three stories. At the time, it was located in a neighborhood of buggy factories. Railroad sidings were critical for plant locations to facilitate shipment of finished automobiles to markets. (BH.)

These eight Model B Buicks, the first production Buicks, lined up on Saginaw Street at First Street in downtown Flint on November 3, 1904. The company had just been placed in the hands of William C. Durant, who would use Buick as the foundation for his creation of General Motors. (BH.)

In 1905, the new management of Olds Motor Works staged the first transcontinental race. Two Curved Dash Runabouts made the trip from New York City to Portland, Oregon, in 44 days. This photo shows the terrible condition of roads (They could hardly be called highways.) in those days. The drivers gave their cars the names "Old Steady" and "Old Scout," like the faithful steeds they were replacing. (OP.)

Two

THE ASSEMBLY

Henry Leland poses here with his pride and joy, the 1905 "telephone booth" Cadillac. By 1908, Cadillac was able to demonstrate the interchangeability of its parts among three different runabout models in an elaborate event staged by a British automobile importer and the Royal Automobile Club. Cadillac won the prestigious Dewar Trophy. Cadillac's success pointed to another fundamental difference between American and European motorcars—that sizable volume also demanded standardized, machine-made parts. This factor gave U.S. autos a distinct service advantage over high-priced, virtually custom-made European motorcars. Cadillac became part of Durant's new General Motors Co. early in 1909. (N.)

Here are 1908 Oldsmobiles, the year when Olds became part of GM, shown in a Boston, Massachusetts dealership. They had grown considerably in size and price from the simple Runabout launched by Olds a few years before, and production had dropped from 5,000 in 1905 to 1,055 three years later. After Durant organized General Motors on September 16, 1908, to merge with Buick, Oldsmobile was his next acquisition on November 12th. Other early members of the infant GM family of cars were Cadillac, Oakland (now Pontiac), Ewing, Marquette, Welch, Scripps-Booth, Sheridan, and Elmore, together with Rapid and Reliance trucks. (N.)

The Oakland of 1908–1909 vintage looked much like the Oldsmobile, except the radiator had a different texture, and the headlamps were mounted higher. This car and crew had been engaged in an unidentified endurance run. Early on, performance events were established as a convincing way to demonstrate a car's reliability and speed, and they continue to this day. Notice that both Olds and Oakland have right-hand drive, which was not uniformly switched to the left side in America until 1915. Oakland became part of GM before the end of 1908. (N.)

This Rapid Truck, a predecessor of GMC truck, climbed Pikes Peak in 1908, the year General Motors was organized. Durant bought several truck companies from 1908 to 1909 and combined them all under the GMC name. The GMC logo was registered on August 1, 1911. Ford Motor Company would have become part of GM in 1908, if Durant had been able to come up with the $2 million in cash demanded by Henry Ford, but New York bankers refused to advance the money. (GA.)

From 1909 to 1919, Buick was easily GM's largest-selling car, speeded by the Model 10. This Buick driver was performing one of the most common tasks of early motorists, changing a tire. Air loss from tires was so common that cars carried more than one spare as well as patch kits and hand air pumps. Easily demountable rims became a popular feature. Note how the motor road ran alongside the rail line, a common positioning of early highways. General Motors' sales for its first full fiscal year ending on September 31, 1909, totaled 25,000 cars and trucks, 19 percent of total U.S. sales. (N.)

This was the Buick plant in Flint about 1912, a facility which continued in production until the summer of 1999. Most workers came to their jobs on foot or in streetcars. The early growth years of the auto industry were akin to that of the personal computer business in the 1980s and 1990s. Buick production exceeded 20,000 in 1910, 60,000 in 1915, and 115,000 in 1919, when it was barely eclipsed by Chevrolet. However, to put that in perspective, Ford's production went from 33,000 in 1910 to 530,000 in 1915 and more than a million in 1919. Buick was GM's big money-maker, selling well overseas as well as in North America. (BH.)

Buick Motor Co. became a mother lode for industry executives. This photo of Buick managers in 1911 included chief engineer Walter L. Marr (second from left), developer of the original Buick production car; works manager Walter P. Chrysler (third from left), who went on to found Chrysler Corporation in 1925; and President Charles W. Nash (fourth from left), who served as GM president from 1912 to 1916 and then created Nash Motors. (BH.)

Charles F. Kettering (1876–1958), who developed the first successful self-starter and became GM's chief of research, tinkers here with a 1913 test Buick in Dayton, Ohio. His Delco (Dayton Engineering Laboratories Co.) firm, purchased for GM by Durant in 1920, grew into the corporation's vast Technical Center and proving grounds in Michigan, Arizona, and overseas. Related businesses growing out of the laboratories were at the core of Delphi Automotive Systems Corp., a GM spin-off in 1999. (GA.)

A hastily drawn sketch was the beginning of a revolution in the automobile industry. This was "Boss" Kettering's original drawing for the patent for the automobile self-starter and ignition system that was introduced on the 1912 Cadillac. Up to that time, cars and trucks had to be started by turning a crank, which was unwieldy, dangerous, and especially discouraging to women motorists. (GW.)

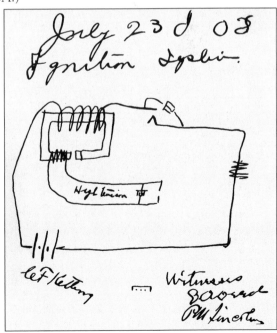

Then as now, automakers used performance events to promote their vehicles. Here was a famous early race driver, Louis Chevrolet (1873–1941), at the wheel of a Buick Model 10 racer in 1910. When Durant decided to start a new car company after he lost control of GM in 1911, he hired the race driver to help design the car and named it after him. Today, no marketer would pick a foreign (French) name, hard to spell and pronounce, for a new model—hence, Chevy. But Durant and his successors, Sloan, Knudsen, and other GM giants, made Chevrolet one of America's icons. (BH.)

In 1912, Louis Chevrolet (standing, left, without hat) had completed two years of development work at the behest of Durant (standing, far right, with derby). Here, they admired the result—the first Chevrolet, a large six-cylinder model. At the wheel was Durant's son, Cliff, with his wife beside him. Chevrolet produced 2,999 vehicles in Detroit in 1912. (GW.)

This 1910 photo of the assembly area at a GM plant (probably Buick) illustrated the high degree of hand labor required to produce early cars. Automobiles of this vintage typically were manufactured from various outside companies' parts: motors, transmissions, axles, wheels, springs, frames, and bodies. Part of Durant's genius lay in combining such firms in "vertical integration" of assembly and marketing companies under the General Motors financial structure. (GA.)

The clothing, office equipment, and furniture in this photo, taken in an unidentified GM executive's office in the early 1900s, provide insight into working lives quite different from those of factory workers, as in the top illustration. (GA.)

"The Oldsmobile Limited"

THE marked difference in wheel diameter, shown by comparison of the tires of the Oldsmobile Limited with those of average size, is a fair measure of the difference between the "Limited" and all other cars . . . In luxurious riding qualities over any kind of surface; in all the elements of "roadability" and in economical maintenance, not only of the car but of the tires as well, the Oldsmobile makes its precedence assured and unassailable.

The silence, power and reliability of the driving mechanism remains unchanged, but in announcing the types for the season of 1910, special attention is called to these important changes in wheel diameters:

all six-cylinder cars have 42 inch wheels
all four-cylinder cars have 36 inch wheels

The four-cylinder Oldsmobile is 40 horse-power, with four speed selective transmission. The wheel base has been increased to 118 inches.
Seven passenger touring cars; two, three and four passenger roadster; toy tonneau and closed cars will be built.

The six-cylinder Oldsmobile is 60 horse-power and will be known as the "Oldsmobile Limited." The seven passenger car is shown above; a roadster body, for two, three or four passengers, will be built on the same chassis. The 1909 edition of this car was oversold and a few early deliveries will be made of the 1910 car, but the year's output is limited.

OLDS MOTOR WORKS, LANSING, MICH.

The 1911 Olds Limited shown in this advertisement was the largest Oldsmobile ever, weighing more than 5,000 pounds and over 16 feet long. It had 42-inch wheels and was powered by a 707-cubic-inch six-cylinder engine producing only 60 horsepower, puny by modern standards. Only 164 were built. (OP.)

The familiar Chevrolet "bow tie" emblem was visible on the radiator of this 1913 model, the first on which it was used. This was also the year Chevrolet Motors moved to Flint and began expanding with smaller, less expensive cars to compete with the Ford Model T. By 1916, Chevrolet's yearly production exceeded 70,000 units. Chevrolet joined GM in 1918. This photo appears to have been taken in a dealer showroom some years later. (N.)

The Fisher brothers were small-town Indiana buggy builders who decided to move to Detroit and get in on the automobile-body manufacturing business. Fisher Body Corp., later for many decades a division of General Motors, was organized in 1908. Here is the original Fisher Body plant in Detroit. The formidable multi-storied building was typical of early auto plants, many designed by Detroit architect Albert Kahn. (GW.)

These painters were laboriously hand-brushing the finishing touches of varnish or top paint on early Fisher bodies, which were, like buggies, constructed of wood. Later, automobile bodies were made of metal formed over wood framing. By the mid-1930s, bodies of mass-production American cars had become all steel. Waiting for paint to dry was a big obstacle to efficient production in the early days of auto production. (GW.)

27

After being president of Buick under Durant, Charles W. Nash (1864–1948) served as the fifth president of General Motors from 1912 to 1916. After leaving GM to make way for Durant's return, he purchased Jeffrey Motors of Kenosha, Wisconsin, and renamed it Nash Motors. Durant became the firm's sixth president and was in office until November 1920. In 1916, the present General Motors Corporation succeeded the original General Motors Company. Although deal-maker Durant had used Chevrolet to regain control of General Motors in 1916, neither Chevrolet nor Canadian operations were consolidated into corporate activities until 1918. (GW.)

This photo of an early GM manufacturing plant illustrates how relatively primitive and labor-intensive machining operations were. Lathes are powered here by belts descending from overhead shafts rather than on-site electricity or electric motors. Compare this to later manufacturing illustrations. (GA.)

These Chevrolets in the Flint, Michigan assembly plant in 1918 were receiving a final check before shipping to customers. By then, left-hand steering had been incorporated. Note that all the units shown here were "rag tops" and used wooden "artillery" wheels. The worker in the foreground is hanging a demountable-rim spare tire on the back of the car. (GA.)

General John J. Pershing, the hero of the Mexican Border campaigns and the commander of U.S. forces in France during World War I, was pictured here with his Cadillac staff car. Because the Motor Age was just getting underway and huge production capacity had yet to be established, Detroit's contribution then was far less than in World War II. However, Henry Leland resigned from Cadillac Motors to start his own company to build aircraft engines. This evolved into Lincoln, which Ford took over in 1922. (GA.)

The Fisher Fleetwood plant on West Jefferson Avenue in Detroit was built in 1917 to manufacture military aircraft. Here is a De Haviland fighter in the plant prior to its delivery to the U.S. government for World War I use. It was renamed the "Liberty," and more than 2,000 were built with a work force of 4,500. The planes were flown away from a vacant field near the plant. (GW.)

One of the earliest recorded examples of women employees in an automotive production facility is shown here, where wooden propellers made at the Fisher aircraft facility were stained and rubbed by women employees. Production hit a high of 40 planes a day. (GW.)

In the year after the First World War ended, General Motors chose this 1919 Oldsmobile to mark the production of its one-millionth car. During the war, Oldsmobile's Lansing plant turned to making Army field-kitchen trailers. Olds car production in 1919 reached 39,000 but declined the following year when a post-war recession set in. (N.)

A forerunner of GM's Frigidaire Division, Guardian Frigerator Co. of Detroit, was purchased by Durant and moved to Dayton in 1918 to integrate with some of Kettering's Delco enterprises, also being brought into GM. The organization produced this first electric refrigerator in Dayton in 1921. Promoted by GM advertising, Frigidaire became the generic name for home refrigerators, even though the device had been developed in 1914 by another Detroit firm, Kelvinator, which later became part of Nash and American Motors Corporation. (GA.)

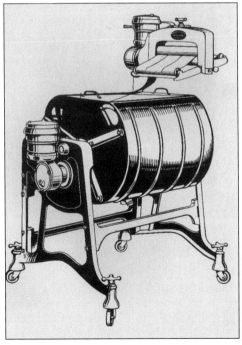

This early GM washing machine, produced by Delco around 1920, is another antecedent of today's many appliances for making household life easier and chores less time-consuming. Washing machines and a long list of other home electric appliances were produced by Frigidaire. The GM division, at one time, also produced air-conditioning units for commercial buildings and portable stand-by generator sets. (GA.)

This experimental tractor was built by GM researchers around 1920. Guidance of the vehicle was by reins to make the transition from horse-drawn farm equipment more acceptable. This tractor was never put into production, although GM did enter the farm implement field for a few years through Durant's 1917–1918 purchases of three companies that became Samson Tractor Division. Today, the legacy of that operation continues with the GM truck plant at Janesville, Wisconsin. (GA.)

By 1920, American automobile firms led an incredible growth industry. Annual production rocketed from 4,200 in 1900 to 187,100 in 1910 and 2,227,000 in 1920. The duPont Company of Delaware, its vaults bursting with profits from making explosives, began investing in GM in 1915, and Pierre S. duPont (1870–1954), left, was elected chairman. When a post-war recession hit in 1920 and vehicle sales were collapsing, Billy Durant's second big whirlwind of purchases from 1916 to 1920 had over-extended the corporation, and crisis set in. GM's stock price plummeted, duPont stepped in, and Durant, right, once again was forced out of GM management—this time forever. (GW.)

Three

BUILDING THE

ORGANIZATION

The General Motors Building, the longtime headquarters of GM, is pictured here during its construction along Detroit's West Grand Boulevard in 1920. Originally designated the Durant Building, it is 15 stories high with 1,320,000 square feet of floorspace and demonstrates Durant's unrestrained optimism for GM growth at a time when the firm held only ten percent of the market and production was about a third that of Ford Motor Company. In contrast, Ford's 1928 administration building in Dearborn included a mere 80,000 square feet. But under duPont control, new concepts of management and products were about to emerge. Coordinated policy was to replace undirected efforts of previous years. (GW.)

Photographed at his desk in 1937, Alfred P. Sloan Jr. was turning over the GM presidency he had held since 1923 to William S. Knudsen (1879–1948), standing, as he became chairman. GM surpassed arch-rival Ford by 1928 as a result of Sloan's brilliant corporate management and vehicle marketing concepts and Ford's ineptness. By the mid-1920s, initial demand for the basic car had been filled. Now car shoppers turned from the venerable Model T and looked for better features and more prestigious models. By the late 1920s, under Sloan and Knudsen, GM had introduced two basic product developments—first, step-up models and second, annual model changes. The latter had the dual purpose of exciting the potential purchaser and rationalizing the introduction of new features, both functional and eye-appealing. Knudsen came to GM from Ford in 1922, built up Chevrolet, and served as president from 1937 to 1940, when he was appointed industrial production chief for national defense in World War II. (GW.)

STAIR-STEP MARKETING

General Motors Prices

Make		August 1, 1922	Make	October 1, 1923
Chevrolet	"490"	$ 510 — $ 860	Chevrolet	$ 490 — $ 795
	"FB"	865 — 1395		
Buick	4	865 — 1395	Oldsmobile 6	750 — 1095
	6	1175 — 2195		
Oakland		975 — 1545	Buick 4	935 — 1495
Oldsmobile	4	1095 — 1745	Oakland	945 — 1395
	8	1495 — 2145	Buick 6	1275 — 2285
Cadillac		3100 — 4600	Cadillac	2985 — 4600

This table shows how GM initiated "stair-step" marketing by readjusting prices and model selection between 1922 and 1923 models. With added-value features to justify carefully layered ascending prices, a ladder was provided from Chevrolet all the way up to Cadillac, the so-called "full line," designed to keep the motorist in the GM family. This evolving price-and-product strategy was supplemented by other GM sales support activities, such as General Motors Acceptance Corporation (GMAC), which financed installment purchases. (D.)

Just when the corporation planned to use Chevrolet to battle Ford in the low-priced market, it became sidetracked by failed efforts to bring a radical, copper-cooled engine to market. Chevrolet did not get its house in order until mid-1923. After this engineering failure, Kettering moved his testing laboratories to Detroit and began a more systematic development of new models and features. By 1925, Chevrolet had more than recovered, as demonstrated by this 100,000th Chevrolet produced in the Janesville, Wisconsin plant—a truck. As shown, it rated a celebration from plant employees. GM also produced its 100-millionth vehicle at the Janesville, Chevrolet plant in 1967. (GA.)

Chevrolet celebrated production of its two-millionth car with this feat of step-climbing dexterity at the state capitol in Jackson, Mississippi. It was common for milestone cars like this one to be sent barn-storming around the country to promote sales. Chevrolet closed the sales gap with Ford by offering more standard features at only slightly higher prices and also was able to supply the public's demand for closed body styles while the T was mainly an open car. (GA.)

Because of the poor reliability of early motor vehicles, availability of good service was a vital aspect of purchase. Many auto service garages evolved from horse-handling liveries, stables, and blacksmiths, as shown in this scene where the blacksmith and his forge are side-by-side with mechanics. Many such early garages quite logically became franchised new car and truck dealers. GM, early on, made a concerted effort to develop supply of parts to, and service training for, both its dealers and independent garages. (GA.)

Pictured here was the first highway coach built by the GMC Truck and Coach Division, the model "Y" of 1925. Outstanding in its day, this coach had a heavy-duty six-cylinder engine, mechanical brakes, leather seats, and window curtains. Buses were far more flexible to serve travelers over short distances than streetcars and interurbans and, in only a few years, revolutionized transit systems in all but the most congested population centers. (GW.)

A 1925 Buick was greeted by a crowd in Moscow's Red Square at the finish of a Leningrad-to-Moscow endurance and reliability run the car won that year. Buicks won four of the five events they entered in the program sponsored by the Soviet government—first prizes for general excellence, economy, speed from a flying start, and speed from a dead start. Export sales were an important aspect of rising U.S. auto and truck production and profits during the 1920s. (BH.)

American makers' success, however, brought on nationalistic trade barriers. Horsepower taxes in several European countries favored the small bore, high-r.p.m. engines typical of small European cars. American geography favored slow-turning, large-cylinder engines for typical long distances. The tax discouraged purchase of American cars by imposing additional annual operating expenses of as much as one-third the purchase price of a Chevrolet. By far the most significant GM overseas activity of 1925, therefore, was the acquisition of Vauxhall Motors of England. Vauxhall was a small producer (1,513 sales in 1926) of large cars like the Tourer, shown above, but gave GM a toehold as a "national" in the home market of the British Empire. Later, it would provide a base for producing small, European-type cars. (N.)

In 1926, GM's Oakland Division introduced the first Pontiac, "a six for the price of a four," as a corporate-directed step-up from the Chevrolet four. The new car made its debut as GM's five-millionth car. Introductory antics to attract customers to dealer showrooms included "wild west" shows with "Indians" (Native Americans) in feathered headdresses. The Pontiac was named for the Michigan city where the Oakland plant and offices were located; the city, in turn, was named for a historical native chief. By this time, the majority of American cars being produced were "all-weather" or closed models, with the proportion rising from 10 percent in 1919 to 85 percent in 1927. Pontiac was GM's first car designed from scratch as a closed car. (GW.)

Here is an old-fashioned employee picnic during the 1920s at GM's New Departure Division in Connecticut. GM employment grew from 14,250 its first year (1908–1909) to 794,000 worldwide at its peak in 1969. At the end of 1998, it was down to 594,000, including 198,000 who were employees of Delphi Automotive Systems, which spun off from the corporation in February 1999. (GA.)

This was one of the few photos existing of all seven Fisher brothers together, taken in 1927 during a groundbreaking ceremony for the Fisher Building in Detroit. From left to right are Alfred J., Lawrence P., Charles T., Fred J., William A., Howard A., and Edward F. Fisher. The brothers were the founders of Fisher Body Corporation, acquired by GM in two steps in 1919 and 1926. Each GM assembly plant had a Fisher Body plant alongside, where bodies were built and interior trim installed before being transferred to the Chevrolet, Oakland/Pontiac, Buick, Oldsmobile, or Cadillac plant for final assembly. (GW.)

Huge fortunes were made, and lost, by entrepreneurs in the auto industry. This is the former home of auto baron Lawrence Fisher (Body by Fisher), on a Detroit River canal, built during the height of the Roaring Twenties. The mansion, a unique blend of Italian Renaissance and Hollywood Vintage architecture, affords a glimpse of the luxuriant lifestyle of one of America's wealthiest families. At the time the mansion was built, Lawrence Fisher was the general manager of Cadillac. (D.)

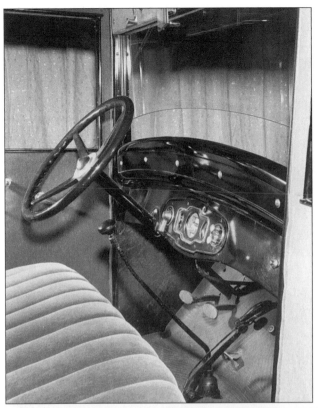

The typical interior and dashboard design of GM's newest car, the 1926 Pontiac, is austere but functional compared to cars of later eras. Note the gear shift lever mounted on the floor and the center "cyclops" instrument cluster, which facilitated the production of cars with either left-hand drive or right-hand drive for export sales. (GA.)

The first LaSalle, a 1927 model shown here, was also the first American production car styled by a professional designer. Harley J. Earl (1893–1969), a longtime GM vice president of styling, came from the West Coast under contract to establish a GM "art and color" section. Previously, engineers built cars, and design followed function. The LaSalle was introduced as a smaller, sportier "companion car" to more expensive Cadillac models. Styling also ushered in the industry practice of annual model changes to stimulate sales. (CH.)

Between 1929 and 1931, GM made its second major overseas purchase—the acquisition of Adam Opel AG of Germany. Founded in 1862 to build sewing machines, Opel became the world's largest bicycle producer, then introduced its first car in 1898. Opel marked its 50,000th car, shown here, in 1928, a year when its relatively modest output of 43,000 still made it Europe's largest automaker. Opel also had a large, modern manufacturing and assembly facility. (N.)

Many of GM's top officials were included in this photograph of GM directors and aides taken in 1928, when they visited Delco-Remy Division at Anderson, Indiana, to approve the production of Delco batteries. From left to right are as follows: (front row) George Whitney, Junius S. Morgan Jr., Alfred P. Sloan Jr. (then president), C. E. Wilson (smiling, then general manager of Delco Remy, later GM president), William S. Knudsen (then a vice president and also subsequently president), Walter S. Carpenter Jr., and R. Samuel McLaughlin; (back row) Charles F. Kettering, Donaldson Brown, Henry M. Crane, John L. Pratt, Charles S. Mott, and Earle F. Johnson. All except Crane and Johnson were directors then. (GW.)

The seemingly easy job of distributing finished cars and trucks to dealerships across the country and around the world has always been one of the biggest headaches for the industry. In the period after 1910, when the industry boomed, rail-line bottlenecks and shortages of rail cars were major obstacles. Special haulaway trucks, like this one carrying 1930 Pontiacs, were developed for trips from assembly plants to dealers within relative short distances, while railroads took auto cargoes on longer cross-country distances. Customers also arranged to visit assembly plants and drive their own new cars home. (GA.)

This 1928 Oldsmobile advertisement in *Ladies Home Journal* used full color as well as descriptions to emphasize the fashionable new styling emanating from GM. It also illustrated the many different body styles sold by Olds. Oldsmobile, however, was hardly a "low price" car, fitting into the middle steps of GM product offerings. (OH.)

Four
REFINEMENT AND TECHNOLOGY

This swanky GM auto "salon," in the ballroom of New York's Old Astor Hotel in January 1930, was a predecessor of GM Motoramas of the 1950s. Brilliant chandeliers and floral displays set off the cars to their best advantage. Although the stock market crash had occurred just a couple of months before, the entire industry had just enjoyed its greatest sales year ever in 1929. Chevrolet had overtaken Ford in 1928 to become the largest selling brand, a position it would hold for most of the rest of the 20th century. And there seemed to be no inkling that a tailspin into the Depression would wipe out many auto producers. New models such as the up-scale Oldsmobile Viking and the down-scale Buick Marquette were being introduced by GM, although in another year, both of these models and the Oakland would be history. (GW.)

The world's first automobile V-16 engine, originally introduced on 1930 Cadillacs, made this custom-bodied 1931 classic touring car a 100-mile-per-hour model. A secondary windshield could be cranked up or down to adjust air flow through the back seat. The car featured steerable cornering lamps in front, and the rear seating compartment provided a speedometer and eight-day clock. But such a high-priced luxury car was ill timed. The production of V-16 Cadillacs, much treasured by wealthy collectors today, was 3,251 from 1930 to 1931 and just 300 in 1932, when the industry hit bottom. During the 1930s, Cadillac also produced V-8 and V-12 models. (CH.)

During 1932, the name of Oakland Motor Car Company was changed to Pontiac Motor Company after GM discontinued the Oakland car. This was the Pontiac division headquarters building on North Saginaw Street in Pontiac for half a century. In the depths of the Depression, to cut costs, GM temporarily combined its three medium-price car divisions into one, called B-O-P (Buick-Olds-Pontiac), a name that was later used for regional assembly plants building models of all three divisions. (D.)

GM's genius of research, "Boss" Kettering, was in charge of a long list of technological developments in the 1920s and 1930s. He is credited with adapting duPont's fast-drying Duco nitrocellulose paint to automotive production, which cut production time and inventories greatly and also provided customers with a variety of colors. His work on engines produced higher power and increased compression ratios from tetraethyl lead additives to gasoline. Before Ethyl, compression ratios typically were four-to-one; afterwards, six- or eight- and ultimately ten-to-one. (GW)

Under Kettering's guidance, GM established the industry's first large-scale proving ground in 1924. Shown here in 1935 is a corner of the then 2,168-acre facility near Milford, 40 miles northwest of Detroit. The test track provided a variety of roads and terrain for secure testing and development of future vehicles. (GW.)

In 1934, General Motors introduced the first successful diesel-powered train in the United States. It was built by GM's Electro-Motive Division and put into service over the Burlington route. At Kettering's recommendation, the corporation acquired several companies struggling to develop large-scale, efficient diesel engines, including Winton of Cleveland, and combined them into what became the world's largest producer of diesel locomotives. The GM locomotives replaced steam engines in only a few years after World War II. (GW.)

As an outgrowth of GM's research and development work with large-scale diesel marine and locomotive engines, in 1939 it introduced this first diesel-powered truck, and a new era in highway freight transportation began. Over the next 40 years, GM diesels came to power medium, heavy, and extra heavy trucks and city and highway buses in both GM and many competitive-make vehicles worldwide. During the 1930s, GM also invested in the aviation industry, owning about 30 percent of North American Aviation and 24 percent of Bendix, a high-tech supplier to the aviation and automotive industries. For a few years, it controlled Eastern Air Lines and TWA. (GW.)

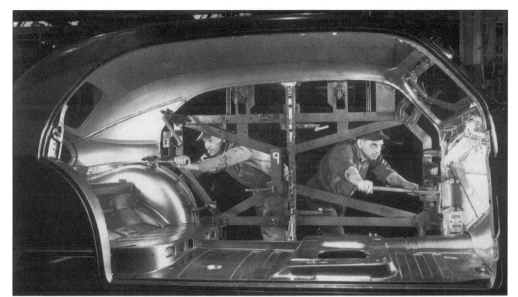

Here, Fisher Body workmen installed the temporary bracing required to position a door pillar before welding it into place on a 1940 Buick "torpedo sedan" body. Today, such work would be handled almost entirely by computer-controlled automatic fixtures and welding guns. GM was not the first to adopt all-steel bodies, but it made the most of its introduction of the steel "turret top" on 1935 models in the fall of 1934. Metallurgical and manufacturing research made it possible to use large pieces of stamped steel for automobile bodies, hoods, and deck-lids. (GW)

No-draft ventilation was considered a major customer-convenience innovation when it was introduced by Fisher Body on GM models in 1933. The installation of these pivoting "quarter windows" replaced leaky crank-out windshields as a means of providing both ventilation and exhaust of tobacco fumes. Automotive air-conditioning and the notion of the "political incorrectness" of accommodating smokers, as in this promotional photo, were years away. (GA.)

This "1935" Cadillac formal sedan was the last Cadillac that did not carry a model-year designation. Many GM sales executives originally opposed the idea of annual model changes, arguing in corporate committees that they preferred bringing on new developments as they were ready, at whatever time. Several other automakers were in agreement, especially Ford. But the public felt otherwise, and automakers had to react. New model cars frequently were posed for promotional photography in elegant residential neighborhoods, as shown here. (CH.)

When Cadillac introduced its 1936 models, illustrated by this snappy convertible coupe, it also moved the time to unveil its new models from January (often in New York) to the fall, as others in the industry already were doing. Fall new-model introductions then prevailed until the 1980s. The styling changes are obvious between the 1935 Cadillac (top) and this 1936, including a split two-piece windshield. (CH.)

This 1936 Pontiac coach was almost at the other end of the scale from Cadillac. Only the Chevrolet, which shared the body shell, would have a lower price. The coach, or two-door sedan, was overwhelmingly the most popular body style for family cars like this, prevailing until after World War II, when hardtops and station wagons gained in popularity. Before the age of seat belts and power door locks, parents feared children would open rear doors and fall out. This was the first year Pontiac adopted its "silver streak" styling, seen in the vertical bright strips on the grille. (PH.)

This smart-looking Opel Kadett, a 1.1-liter "cabrio-coach," was introduced in 1936 at the Paris Auto Show, shown here. As the German economy improved during the 1930s, GM's investment in Opel flowered. But the Nazi regime would not allow GM to send any of its profits home. Consequently, Opel reinvested heavily in new passenger car and light truck models, which also were exported successfully to non-auto producing countries in Europe as well as to Latin America, Africa, and the Far East. (N.)

The All-American Soap Box Derby was sponsored, beginning in 1934, by Chevrolet in cooperation with dealers and local newspapers, civic groups and broadcast stations. Here is Derby Downs, a 975-foot course in Akron, Ohio, where the finals were run each year before crowds as big as 70,000. In one of American industry's greatest promotional programs, some 60,000 boys between the ages of 11 and 15 each year designed, built, and raced wooden "soap box cars" based on packing cases and toy wagon wheels. Well into the 1960s, arch-rival Ford sought a comparable program where throngs of parents could be drawn into dealerships to obtain soap-box entry forms—and sales pitches. The Soap Box Derby continues today on a reduced scale. GM withdrew from its participation around 1970. (GA.)

As the Depression wore on and social consciousness rose during the New Deal years, union organizing drives came to the auto industry. The United Auto Workers (UAW) chose to take on General Motors on December 28, 1936, when workers refused to leave their posts at a Cleveland plant. It was called a "sit-down strike" and was highly controversial because, from GM's point of view, it was an illegal take-over of corporate property. From the union viewpoint, it blocked vital General Motors production while preventing employment of strike-breaking non-union workers. The strike spread to Fisher Body Plant No. 1 in Flint, adjacent to the Chevrolet assembly plant, where workers were shown here relaxing on automobile seats intended for installation in the car bodies in the background. (R.)

The strike grew ugly in Flint when crowds massed in support of workers inside, wrecking police cars and smashing windows. Widespread injury was feared, and the Michigan governor called in hundreds of armed National Guard troops to prevent violence and protect property. After 44 days, General Motors capitulated and signed its first contract with the UAW. (R.)

One of the most advanced production models ever introduced was the 1938 Cadillac Fleetwood Sixty Special, unveiled at the New York automobile exposition. Built only as a top-of-the-line touring sedan, the Sixty Special presented several pioneering design concepts—the elimination of running boards for wider, six-passenger interior; an extended rear deck; a lowered belt line; front-hinged rear doors; and no door frames around the windows—all two years ahead of the adoption of many of these features on other GM cars. (CH.)

The original "dream car" designed by Harley Earl and introduced by GM in 1938 to test reaction to advanced ideas was this famous Buick "Y-Job." It was 10 years ahead of its time and began a long parade of dramatic "dream cars" by GM and other automakers worldwide, continuing today. Buick adopted this car's "waterfall" grille design beginning with 1942 models, used it for many years after the war, and has returned to it as a "signature" in recent years. (BH.)

This front shot of the 1938 Buick showed off some of the best "art deco" GM design of the period, with wide-spaced horizontal grille bars, impressive high-mounted headlight pods, "streamlining" decoration on hood sides, and a stylized emblem on the bumper. The photo was from the "reference" file of another manufacturer, donated to a public library collection when it no longer had relevance for competitive purposes. GM stylists had to develop entirely different appearances for each of GM's six car lines, several of which shared common sheet metal and bodies. (N.)

The 1938 Buick was one of the first cars to adopt steering-column mounting for the gear shift lever, as shown here, moving it from the floor. This freed the front seat to be comfortable for three people. Note the spacious interior, typical of the time, with plenty of room upwards for the hats men and women commonly wore then and lots of space to sit in the back even with a passenger's knees crossed. Rear floor space was ample enough to act as a child's playpen. (N.)

Vauxhall sales climbed from 2,587 in 1928 to 59,746 in 1937, while Opel's went from 42,771 to 128,370 over the same period. With forced reinvestment, Opel brought out two new six-cylinder models just before the war, the 3.6-liter Admiral for 1938, shown here as a four-door convertible sedan, and the 2.5-liter Kapitan for 1939. All these cars featured styling more advanced than GM's North American cars. For example, headlamps were mounted integrally in the hood or fenders. (N.)

Looking more like a 1939 Chrysler product than a GM car, the 1939 Opel 2.5-liter Kapitan featured an all-steel integral body, synchronized transmission, four-wheel hydraulic brakes, and a new 55-horsepower 150-cubic-inch overhead-valve short-stroke six-cylinder engine. In contrast, the 1939 Chevrolet was powered by an 85-horsepower, 216.5-cubic-inch overhead-valve Six. Opel also had introduced, in 1935, an advanced four-main-bearing overhead-valve over-square-design four-cylinder engine for its smaller cars. (N.)

Here is a conservatively styled 1939 Vauxhall 12, exported from Britain to Argentina, where it was photographed participating in an endurance run. To put GM's European operations in perspective, in 1932 Opel's production exceeded that of Oldsmobile and the following year, nearly matched Buick; in 1936, it was almost double that of GM-Canada. Two years later, Opel's production of 140,580—a full line of several cars for different markets plus the Blitz truck—surpassed Oldsmobile's 93,706 and Pontiac's 95,108, both deeply cut by a domestic recession in 1938. Vauxhall's war-swelled Bedford truck output of 54,696 units in 1940 approached GMC's 61,660. (GA.)

This 1938 Chevrolet was the 100,000th car assembled by GM in South Africa and is a right-hand-drive model. Chevrolet had a large export operation in New Jersey to box incompletely assembled vehicles that were shipped overseas for final assembly with varying amounts of local content, such as glass, upholstery, tires, and sometimes entire bodies. Most right-hand-drive cars and trucks, primarily for the British Empire, were supplied from GM's Canadian plants. (GA.)

This Chevrolet dealership in St. Petersburg, Florida, in 1937, was typical of pre-war U.S. retail outlets. GM had a peak of 17,360 domestic car and truck dealers in 1941 with average dealership sales of 107 new vehicles yearly and total employment of 190,000. After World War II, the trend was to a smaller number of dealerships, which on average were larger. Dealer sales averaged 222 new units in boom-year 1955 and nearly 300 in the early 1960s, when GM's U.S. dealership employment reached 275,000. (N.)

As promoted in this advertisement, 1940 Oldsmobiles introduced Hydra-Matic, the first completely automatic (clutchless) transmission. After successful launching with Olds, Hydra-Matic became an option in Cadillac for 1941 and Pontiac for 1948. In parallel, GM Research developed torque-converter type automatics for Buick (1948 model) and Chevrolet (1950 model). Thus, GM led the industry in development of completely automatic transmissions to make driving easier. (OP.)

56

Visitors to the General Motors Highways and Horizons exhibit at the New York World's Fair in 1939 were given a remarkably prophetic glimpse of today's Interstate Highway system with this miniature scale layout of a highway intersection. Excited as they were by this "dream," few ever imagined such highways would become reality in less than 20 years. One of the nation's first limited-access highways, the Merritt Parkway through congested southern Connecticut, opened its first stretch in summer 1938, and work on the Pennsylvania Turnpike started late that fall. (GW.)

Automotive history was made on January 11, 1940, when GM produced its 25-millionth production car. The scene was the Chevrolet assembly plant in Flint, and all GM'S top officials were on hand. Among the notables pictured, to the right of the car, are M.E. Coyle, general manager of Chevrolet; W.S. Knudsen, president of GM; Alfred P. Sloan Jr., chairman; and C.E. Wilson, executive vice president. (GW.)

Cadillac's 1941 model marked the last of the custom-bodied cars typical of the early and classical-car days of the industry, as illustrated by this rare convertible limousine. At one time, luxury car buyers could order a chassis from the factory and have it shipped to a body company for installation of such a custom body. By 1941, GM accounted for 44 percent of total U.S. auto sales, compared with 12 percent in 1921. (D.)

This 1941 Cadillac Series 62 four-door convertible sedan ended the availability of such factory-produced body styles from General Motors. The year before, Cadillac had discontinued the LaSalle, substituting a lower-priced Cadillac 61 model. As a result, for 1941—the best year for the industry since 1929—Cadillac sales climbed to a then-record of 41,435. GM's volume leader Chevrolet achieved 1941 output of 930,293, compared to Ford's 600,814. (D.)

Five

ARSENAL OF DEMOCRACY

When the United States was drawn into World War II on December 7, 1941, General Motors already had a head start on defense work. ("Defense" was the word used before America declared war; afterwards it was "war" production.) From the mid-1930s, GM had been developing high performance aircraft through its control of North American Aviation, the producer of AT-6 training planes, P-51 fighters, and B-25 bombers. GM president "Bill" Knudsen, a Danish immigrant, resigned in September 1940 to take charge of defense production for the nation. This photo from February 3, 1942, shows the last Buick built before the Flint factory was converted to World War II military production. Although civilian car production was halted, thousands of 1941 and 1942 model passenger sedans had been purchased by the military for use as staff cars. (BH.)

Predictably, GM's largest contribution to the war effort was the production of vehicles—38,000 tanks and 854,000 trucks—including this unique amphibious model, nicknamed the "Duck," which was indispensable for supporting beach invasions. The Duck was developed by GMC Truck and Coach Division, could travel on land and water, and participated in landings from Normandy to Iwo Jima. GMC medium trucks became the Allied Armies' most famous troop and cargo mover, the ubiquitous "Six by Six." (GW.)

A notable GM effort was the production of Grumman Wildcat fighters and Avenger torpedo bombers for the U.S. Navy. This former B-O-P assembly plant in New Jersey built 7,546 of these Avengers, more than the parent Grumman company built. Elsewhere, GM produced more than 5,000 Wildcats. Former U.S. President George W. Bush was piloting a GM-built Avenger when he was shot down in the Pacific as a young Navy officer during the war. (GW.)

GM's Allison Engine Division in Indianapolis developed the famous V-1710 liquid-cooled aircraft engine, which made a major contribution during World War II. Among the military aircraft it powered were the famous twin-tailed P-38 Lightning long-range fighter, shown here, as well as the P-40 of Flying Tiger fame, the rear-engined P-39 Airacobra, and the P-43 King Cobra night-fighter. Altogether, GM supplied 206,000 aircraft engines for the Air Force, one-fourth of all the aircraft engines America produced for the war effort. (GW.)

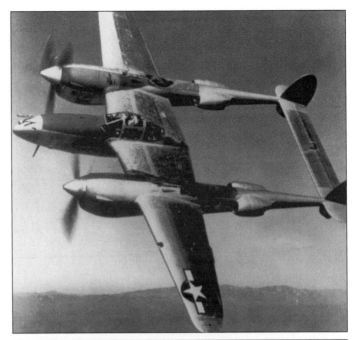

Here is a typical wartime assembly line scene in a General Motors plant. In place of shiny automobiles, these Chevrolet light military trucks rolled from assembly lines together with mountains of other war materials. For example, GM supplied 198,000 diesel engines for use primarily in tanks and landing craft; Pontiac built Oerlikon 20-mm anti-aircraft cannons; .30-caliber light machine guns were supplied by Saginaw Steering Gear Division; and Frigidaire turned out some 327,000 .50-caliber heavy machine guns. (GA.)

At war's end in 1945, GM found both its Opel plant at Russelsheim, Germany, shown here, and GM Continental assembly plant at Antwerp, Belgium, had been badly damaged by Allied air attacks in 1943 and 1944. The Vauxhall plant at Luton, England, was bombed in 1940 by the German Luftwaffe with a loss of 39 employees but not seriously damaged. GM Limited's Southampton, England plant was damaged in a 1941 bombing. The smashed car at the Opel plant is a 1936-vintage Opel 2-liter, the German company's top-of-the-line model in the mid-1930s. (GA.)

Shown in 1942, Alfred P. Sloan Jr. (left) and Charles F. Kettering were two longtime GM business colleagues who established the Sloan-Kettering Institute for Cancer Research in 1945. Charles S. Mott (1875–1973), right, for many years GM's largest single stockholder, was an axle manufacturer in Utica, New York, who moved his business, later part of GM, to Flint in 1906. He created the Mott Foundation principally to help his adopted city of Flint. (GA.)

Six
POST-WAR RECOVERY

After World War II, Oldsmobile provided specially equipped cars to disabled veterans and others with debilitating injuries. Known as "Valiants," some 26,000 of these cars were built with clutchless automatic transmissions and other devices that enabled operation even by people with severe disabilities. Disabled veterans received an allowance from the federal government to cover the purchase. A 1947 Oldsmobile 66 sedan with Hydra-Matic had a factory price of about $1,500. (OP.)

Quick to pick up postponed pre-war plans, GM announced it would build a huge new Technical Center north of Detroit in Warren, Michigan. Here, at a luncheon in New York on July 24, 1945, top GM officials examined a scale model of the Tech Center. (GA.)

GM's first vehicle produced post-war, on August 20, 1945, was a 1946 Chevrolet truck similar to the one shown at left. There was a huge, round-the-world, pent-up demand for cars—and especially trucks—due to the four to six years' missed production, vehicles that were lost to war damage or worn out, and the accumulated cash available to make purchases. The 1948 Buick "woody" station wagon, at right, was equipped with one of the first new technical developments in the post-war period—the "Dynaflow" torque-converter automatic transmission, which was introduced for top-of-the-line Roadmaster models. (D.)

Though hindered by severe material shortages and government controls, Vauxhall switched quickly to civilian vehicles when hostilities ceased. By the end of 1945, 32,471 Bedford trucks had been built, and passenger car output was about to begin. Shown here is one of the first post-war Vauxhall cars, a Model 10. Vauxhall's production in 1949 totaled 83,147 vehicles, substantially more than the best pre-war levels of about 60,000. (N.)

With a 1929 Buick and a 1948 Chevrolet, M.E. Coyle, then a GM executive vice president, demonstrated to members of a Congressional committee in 1948 how GM increased the value of its cars over the years. The chart compared prices, features, and performance of the two cars, produced nearly 20 years apart. The Congressional interest probably grew out of a long post-war strike by the UAW against GM and rapidly increasing prices during an inflationary period. (GA.)

In 1947, the streamlined GM Train of Tomorrow, built by Electro-Motive Division as a "contribution to forward thinking of American railroads," began a two-and-a-half-year tour of North America. Spectacular "AstroDome" cars introduced on the Train of Tomorrow became standard on cross-country passenger railroads. As shown in this photo taken a wintry day somewhere in the Midwest, the Train of Tomorrow attracted large crowds. It also helped convince railroads to replace steam engines with modern diesels. (GA.)

Powered by an efficient, reliable truck diesel, the standard GM city transit bus, shown here on a Pontiac street about 1949, became America's most familiar means of urban transit in the post-war years. Most traditional bus makers withdrew from the market, and even new electric street cars, tied to their inflexible rails and facing suburban population growth far beyond their lines, could not compete. GM also did a huge export business with its diesel coaches. (N.)

Announced in the fall of 1945 and introduced to the public on November 29, 1948, the Holden represented GM's third great manufacturing center overseas and the first in the Pacific. Until this, all GM's overseas plants besides Vauxhall and Opel were assembly, small-parts-production, or warehousing operations. The first Holden, shown here coming off the assembly line, was as a four-cylinder, four-place, four-door sedan larger than Vauxhalls being imported from Britain but smaller than the Chevrolet, which it resembled except for its Buick-like grille. (N.)

Opel had been GM's largest overseas producer and also the worst damaged by the war. Opel employees sought permission from American occupation authorities to commence civilian production and completed a Blitz 1.5-liter truck on July 15, 1946. Production of the pre-war four-cylinder Olympia passenger car shown here began in December 1947. Initially, GM's corporate management debated whether the Opel plant was worth taking back, as American military authorities urged. A GM study group early in 1948 recommended resumption of control, only to be turned down by the financial policy committee. Fortunately, GM chairman Alfred P. Sloan Jr. overruled the committee by proposing a two-year probationary period for Opel under GM aegis. Accordingly, Opel again became part of the corporation, and GM repaid the U.S. taxes owed from the wartime write-off of Opel assets. (N.)

In 1948, GM presented its first new post-war design, the sensational Cadillac Sixty Special, shown here with "tail fins" modeled after the Lockheed P-38 fighter plane. Because fins were non-functional, except for hiding the gas cap on some models, social critics heaped criticism on them. But the public obviously appreciated what they perceived as the futuristic look. Fins remained part of Cadillac styling until 1964 and were widely copied by virtually every other make in the American industry and many overseas. (CH.)

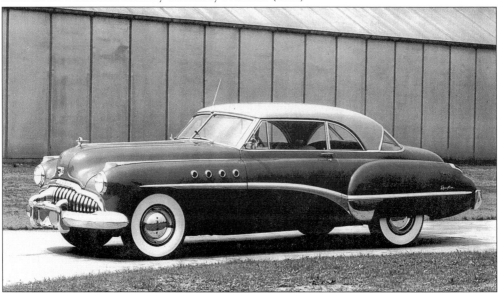

Another much-copied and popular GM styling innovation in the post-war period was the so-called hardtop coupe, pioneered on this 1949 Buick Roadmaster Riviera model. More properly named a "pillarless" sedan by European observers, the hardtop gave the sporty, open feeling of a convertible without the added cost and limited durability of the convertible top. (N.)

Seven

MASTERY OF THE
BUYER'S MARKET

The Buyer's Market, which replaced the Seller's Market in the 1950s, was symbolized by Oldsmobile's 303-cubic-inch, 135-horsepower Rocket V8 Engine introduced in 1948 on 1949 models. It was a high-compression, high-performance engine, the first of its kind in the industry, and evolved from development on tank engines during World War II. Oldsmobile production increased from 178,000 1947 models to 288,000 1949s. Cadillac's standard engine was a slightly larger, more powerful version at 331 cubic inches and 160 horsepower. By 1955, all other American makes were offering similar overhead-valve, high compression V-8s. With its sensational performance, Olds swept stock car races and the romantic Mexican Road Race, while Cadillac entered the famous LeMans race in France, an unusual role for a luxury sedan. Cadillac finally began to overtake Packard, which went out of business in less than a decade. (OP.)

After a hiatus of several years, in 1950, GM returned to New York with its own "auto show," the first of several private GM "Motoramas," dramatic showmanship for displaying new and "teaser" products. This "clover leaf" with five turntables—one for each car line—was built for the Motorama, and is shown here in New York's Waldorf-Astoria Hotel, where it made its debut before traveling elsewhere around the country. (GA.)

Despite a ragged past with the United Auto Workers, the corporation reached a historic five-year pact with the union in 1950, freeing it from strike threats. Led by UAW president Walter P. Reuther (1907–1970), in the vest, union leaders cheerily signed the agreement with GM officials. Reuther, a charismatic leader and persuasive bargainer, was reluctantly respected for his socialist idealism, which kept the union honest, and his foresight in ejecting Communists from the UAW when he took control in 1946. Reuther had risen in the UAW's General Motors Department after once being a Ford die-maker. (GA.)

The Korean War, which broke out in June 1950, again required the auto industry to supply defense materials. This photo of the final assembly line at the Cadillac tank plant was taken in 1951. GMC once again cranked out its famous "Six-By" two-and-a-half-ton military trucks. Turning to defense production was more taxing this time because civilian demand for passenger cars and trucks also was rising rapidly, testing GM's and the industry's capacity to serve both needs. (GA.)

This photo was taken in 1953, when the Harlow H. Curtice, right, became General Motors' 11th president. Curtice was elected when Charles E. Wilson (1890–1961), left, resigned to become President Eisenhower's secretary of defense. Wilson became known in Washington as "engine Charlie" to distinguish him from another Charles Wilson, a top executive of General Electric. (GA.)

A spectacular fire on August 12, 1953, destroyed GM's Detroit Transmission Division Plant in Livonia, Michigan, cutting off production of Hydra-Matic. The fire halted assembly of new Cadillacs, Oldsmobiles, and Pontiacs, as well as competitors Lincoln, Nash, Hudson, and Kaiser, which bought the automatic transmission from GM. On October 21, 1953, just 60 working days after the fire, the first Hydra-Matic was produced in a temporary plant following a gigantic movement of machines and tools. (GA.)

As Britain and the Continent slowly recovered from the war, GM's overseas affiliates began to come out with all-new models, just as in America. This is a 1952 Vauxhall Vector model, far different in appearance from the stodgy, warmed-over 1930s models first offered in the late 1940s. Opel likewise introduced modern designs after 1950. (N.)

On July 3, 1952, medical history was made in Detroit with the first successful substitution of a mechanical heart during surgery, shown here, on a 41-year-old man. The mechanism was developed cooperatively by surgeons of Harper Hospital and GM Research engineers. Later, the original model was put on permanent display at the Smithsonian Institution in Washington, D.C. It was one of several contributions to medical science by GM researchers. (GA.)

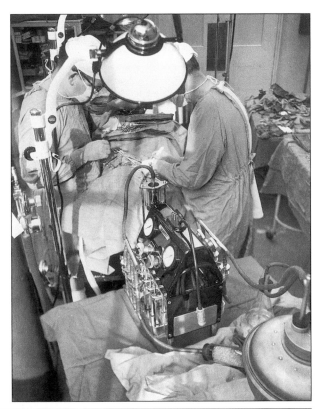

The Euclid Division (later designated TEREX Division) joined the GM family through acquisition in 1953. Previously, GM had been supplying the earth-moving equipment firm with diesel engines. This twin-powered scraper with diesel engines at each end self-loaded up to 32 cubic yards at a time. It was a timely purchase for GM, antedating the start of the massive interstate highway system project by less than five years. Strategic dispositions during the decade of the 1980s by GM began with the sale of TEREX to a European company. (GA.)

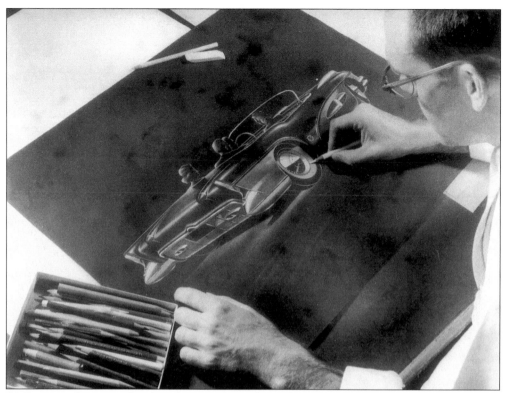

GM's original caption for this photograph in the early 1950s was as follows: "Here a young designer at GM Styling practiced sketching a possible new model—one of the techniques used in early stages of automotive design. Out of such sessions at the drawing board come the ideas that will be selected for production cars of the future." And actually the rear end came to resemble the 1956 Buick. (GA.)

For 1953, Cadillac introduced the Eldorado, shown here, as a limited-edition convertible. It was the first production model to utilize one of GM's worst styling ideas, the wraparound windshield with its "dog-leg" front pillar, known also as a knee-knocker. The public liked it, though, and even as it spread to other GM cars, Ford hastened to copy it. More conservative Chrysler, however, held back, and its sales suffered. The Eldorado also had cut-down doors like the pre-war Darrin custom-bodied cars of various makes. Buick offered a similar model, called the Skylark. Both are much treasured by collectors today. (CH.)

In the 1950s, GM anticipated the Buyer's Market by introducing new customer conveniences as well as styling innovations. This publicity photo—probably of a 1955 model—illustrates the power steering unveiled on the 1952 Cadillac, Buick, and Oldsmobile. For 1953, Chevrolet and Pontiac offered it as an extra-cost option as well. It made a special hit with women and, when later offered on heavy trucks, was a boon to truck drivers also. (GA.)

When it was first shown as a "dream car" at one of GM's Motoramas, the Corvette created a sensation. Chevrolet rushed to get it into production, even though the only engine available was Chevy's bread-and-butter OHV Six, jazzed up for the first 'Vette with quirky triple-carburetion. Production began in 1953 by Chevrolet on the Corvette, a "dream car" which became the industry's first production car with a fiberglass body. Here, a GM engineer held the car's plastic floorpan in the air to demonstrate its light weight. (GA.)

Shifting gears on the nation's trucks as they rolled the highways was once an onerous task. In 1954, GMC Truck and Coach Division became first in the industry to offer automatic transmissions for every-sized truck, as shown here. This was a milestone in GM's history and an engineering advance that meant greater control and ease of handling for truck drivers. Truck automatics were produced by the Allison Division, maker of World War II fighter-plane engines. (GA.)

GM's diesel locomotives were mass-produced on automobile-like assembly lines. Here, cab ends for GM diesel passenger and freight locomotives are shown at the Electro-Motive Division plant in LaGrange, Illinois. GM came to dominate the American locomotive market and, by 1962, had delivered more than 2,500 of its railroad diesels to 35 countries outside North America as well. (GA.)

On the right is the world's first room air conditioner, built by GM's Frigidaire Division in 1929. At left is Frigidaire's 25th anniversary model built in 1954. The newer, more efficient model sold for half as much as its predecessor. Frigidaire had built nearly 600,000 room air conditioners by the time of the corporation's 50th birthday in 1958. (GA.)

GM's treatment of women in publicity photographs in the 1950s reflected the times but might be considered sexist today. Here is what the original caption said: "At AC Spark Plug Division, employees choose a queen from their ranks each year and there's plenty of beauty from which to choose. This shows Barbara Cooke, winner, and her court—all finalists." The reality was, GM salaried employees, including executives, enjoyed many employment benefits, some of them first bargained for hourly workers by the UAW. A GM job—or a Ford or Chrysler job—was considered a good job, and multiple generations of families, men and women, have worked in the industry. (GA.)

This scene in a General Motors manufacturing plant of the late 1950s demonstrated how master mechanics, tool and machine designers, plant layout men, and supplier firms had radically changed auto plants since the early days of the industry. Compare this photo, for instance, with the *c.* 1915 view on page 28. Today, such a scene would be equally changed by computer controls and robotic devices. (GA.)

Changing tastes in casual clothing are reflected in this scene at a picnic held by GMC Truck and Coach Division employees in the 1950s. Compare it to the New Departure Division picnic around 1925 shown on page 38. Improvements in working conditions, compensation, and fringe benefits by the late 1950s, many union-negotiated, would have seemed beyond the dreams of those workers in the 1920s. GM and industry prosperity made it possible. (GA.)

On November 23, 1954, GM's 50-millionth U.S.-made vehicle rolled off the Chevrolet assembly line in Flint, Michigan. Fittingly, its hardware was gold-plated. Flint staged a civic celebration in honor of the event. The top-of-the-line Chevrolet BelAire two-door hardtop chosen as the landmark vehicle was all-new for 1955 and introduced the well-regarded small-block Chevy V-8. Chevrolet began sponsoring the weekly Dinah Shore musical variety review on network television. Every show, she sang the unforgettable Chevy theme song, "See the USA in your Chevrolet." (GA.)

Thousands cheered as General Motors' 50-millionth car rode through Flint on a float in a mile-long ceremonial parade marking the event. In addition to the parade and a ceremony at the assembly plant, civic luncheons were held in 65 cities from coast to coast, and GM plants held open house across the country to more than a million people. (GA.)

The 1955 Oldsmobile introduced the industry's first four-door hardtop, shown here, following in GM's tradition of giving Olds a shot at corporation "firsts." The new body style, widely copied in subsequent years by competitors, also was offered by Buick that first year. During the 1950s, the combination of the "Rocket V8" with "Futuramic" styling propelled Oldsmobile into first place in the medium-price field and fourth in industry sales. (N.)

Here, in an informal photo taken at the opening of GM's 1956 Motorama in New York, are three of the four presidents who guided GM from 1923 to 1958. From left to right were Harlow H. Curtice, president of GM from 1953 to 1958; Alfred P. Sloan Jr., president from 1923 until 1937 and chairman when this photo was made; and Charles E. Wilson, GM president from 1941 until 1953 when he left to become secretary of defense, the position he held when this photo was made. A few months later, Sloan retired from active management. (GA.)

Model year 1956 was the last when Pontiac styling still utilized the "silver streak" theme first adopted 20 years before. This showed a Pontiac wagon in a studio preparatory to promotional photography. All-steel station wagons were the typical family vehicle of the 1950s, replacing the two-door coach of the 1920s and 1930s and barely anticipating the minivans of the 1980s and Sports Utility Vehicles of the 1990s. (PH.)

The Allison turbo-jet engine in the foreground and the McDonnell airframe in the background teamed up in the 1950s to produce a powerful fighting plane for the Carrier Task Forces of the U.S. Navy. GM continued to support extensive defense production during the Cold War. (GA.)

Five thousand distinguished guests attended the dedication shown here of GM's $100,000,000 Technical Center north of Detroit on May 16, 1956. Closed-circuit television carried it to thousands more across the U.S. Plans to build the Tech Center had first been announced more than ten years before. (GW.)

Automakers long had been fundamentally concerned with vehicle safety as they progressively installed such features as laminated safety glass, improved tires and brakes, and all-steel bodies. In the mid-1950s, however, they became aware through research at Cornell and Northwestern Universities of crash-related injuries from interiors and ejection from the vehicle. In 1956, Ford introduced a "safety package" of dash padding, improved door locks, and seat belts; others quickly followed. This shows a research barrier crash of a 1956 Chevrolet at GM's Milford Proving Ground as part of a demonstration for a Congressional committee. (GW.)

As North America developed into a major market for European imported cars in the late 1950s, GM adopted the rational policy of offering Opel through Buick dealers and Vauxhall through Pontiac in the U.S. The Opel-Buick connection continued into the 1970s, when it was finally abandoned due to a combination of factors. Here, GM president Harlow H. Curtis and Carl H. Kindl, then vice president in charge of Canadian and Overseas Operations, stand behind an Opel Caravan as it was announced in 1957 for the American market. (GW.)

American Pontiac dealers sold this English-built Vauxhall Victor for several years beginning in the fall of 1957. By careful planning, this model, aimed mainly at the British market, closely resembled the American Pontiac in styling, although smaller. (N.)

Twenty-nine of the 36 members of GM's Board of Directors posed for this photograph at the GM Technical Center on September 5, 1957. The board then included at least 19 active or retired GM executives and representatives of major investment groups and banks. This is in marked contrast to the much smaller, diverse, and predominantly "outsider" GM Board of 1999, which has only 15 members, including just three members of GM management. (GA.)

This aerial view of Fisher Body No. 1 plant in Flint, site of the infamous 1937 sit-down strike, typified the 126 GM plants throughout the United States when GM celebrated its 50th anniversary in 1958. This plant supplied bodies to the nearby Chevrolet assembly plant. (GA.)

By the late 1950s, GM had become a major factor in the home appliance industry, as shown in this photograph of a model kitchen including a Frigidaire range, dishwasher, and refrigerator. Elsewhere in the home would have been a Frigidaire washer, dryer, and air conditioning. Yet the business suffered a decline and unprofitable competition in the decades following, so GM sold Frigidaire to White Consolidated Industries in 1979 after producing over 100 million Frigidaire appliances. (GA.)

In 1958, GM designer Peggy Sauer was pictured "helping style ultra modern interiors including dashboards." Female professional and management employees in the auto industry were few and far between until the last two decades of the 20th century. GM claimed to pioneer the use of women designers on its Styling Staff "in recognition of woman's tremendous influence on car purchases," but Studebaker had hired a woman designer in 1935. (GA.)

In addition to mastering the market for city transit buses with its superior technology, GM also developed highly competitive highway coaches, such as this 1950s Scenicruiser. It featured an observation deck, air conditioning, foam rubber recliner seats, air suspension ride, tinted glare-resistant window glass, and a lavatory, great improvements over the 1925 bus shown on page 36. (GW.)

The most novel "dream cars" developed by GM in the 1950s were these three jet- or turbine-powered Firebirds, shown at GM's Arizona Proving Ground in 1958 with Harley Earl, then vice president in charge of Styling Staff. Firebird I, left, was introduced at the 1954 Motorama as the first gas-turbine vehicle built and tested in the U.S. Firebird II, center, was the first gas turbine passenger car suitable for highway use, introduced by GM in 1956. Firebird III, called the first "space age inspired car," was the star of GM's 1959 Motorama. Among its many features was a single stick control system to replace the steering wheel, brake pedal, and accelerator. (GA.)

In the courtyard of GM Styling at the Tech Center, Harley Earl posed with GM's 50th anniversary 1958 passenger cars. Earl supervised the design of more than 35 million cars during his career with GM, which began in 1927. A 1958 Chevrolet Impala is in the foreground. Behind it, from left to right, are a Pontiac, Oldsmobile, Buick, and Cadillac. (GW.)

This 1950s scene of employees changing shifts at a GM plant was typical for the corporation's plants in 70 U.S. cities, plus six facilities in Canada and manufacturing operations in 16 other countries. GM's golden anniversary hit in the midst of an industry-wide recession, with slow sales and sharply reduced production. However, the UAW had negotiated a company-funded "supplemental unemployment benefit" on top of government benefits for North American auto workers, which greatly eased the economic impact of layoffs. (GW.)

Stock car auto racing became a corporate sporting event for the auto industry in the 1950s, with practically every make competing with factory support for checkered flags. Lee Petty is shown here with the '59 Oldsmobile race car in which he won the first Daytona 500-mile race in 1959. (DIS and OH.)

GM led the styling trend in the 1950s to longer, lower, and wider cars, with Easter-egg-colored exteriors and interiors, both amply adorned with bright metal decoration. The 1959 Cadillac Eldorado convertible, shown here with cartoon-inspiring tailfins, typified the decade and a car culture that was about to change. Now, the 1959 Cadillac has achieved a cult status all its own as a true icon of the decade. (CH.)

Eight
EXTERNAL INFLUENCES

A technological wonder among mass-production American cars, this '60 Chevrolet Corvair was introduced in 1959 as GM's response to the successful bridgehead established in U.S. markets by the rear-engined VW Beetle. The Corvair had a rear-mounted, aluminum-block, air-cooled six-cylinder engine and built a loyal owner following. But it fell victim to consumer advocate and Washington lawyer Ralph Nader, who accused the Corvair of being "unsafe at any speed," the title of his book attacking GM and the industry. Ford and Chrysler introduced more conventional "compact" cars that were relatively more successful in sales. However, Chevrolet correctly maintained that the Corvair did not cannibalize sales of full-sized cars, whereas its competitors' approach did. Thus the 1960s ushered in marketing strategy battles, overshadowed by the threat of Washington. Unlike production assistance supporting America's previous war efforts earlier in the century, the auto industry was little involved in the Vietnam War. (N.)

For the following model year, 1961, GM's "medium-priced divisions" introduced their own compact cars, typified by the Buick Special, shown here, along with the Oldsmobile F-85 and Pontiac Tempest. Each had unconventional product features. Buick and Olds shared an aluminum block V-8, and Pontiac incorporated a "half-eight" slant four with a rear-mounted transmission—called a transaxle—connected with a flexible drive shaft. The important point, apparently unseen by many at the time, was that Sloan's magic, clearly delineated "stair-step" product-and-market system was thus violated by the new size and price entries. (N.)

When the public appeared to want a more conventional small car than the Corvair, Chevrolet crashed for two years to bring out this 1962 Chevy II, in many respects almost a carbon copy of the Ford Falcon. The Chevy II proved to be far more popular with conventional Chevrolet customers than the Corvair. It was during this period that Chevrolet's advertising agency came up with another unforgettable theme: "Baseball, hot dogs, apple pie and Chevrolet." (N.)

When former GM president Bill Knudsen's son, Semon "Bunkie" Knudsen, became general manager of Pontiac in 1956, he resolved to build a new product-based image for the make. For the 1959 model, the track—the distance across the car between wheels—was widened by 4.5 to 4.9 inches, and an advertising campaign extolling the roadability of Pontiac "wide-track" design was launched. Pontiac sales soared. This white Pontiac convertible rolled into history at the division's plant in Pontiac, Michigan, on March 14, 1962, to become GM's 75-millionth U.S.-made vehicle. (GA.)

The introduction of GM "mid-sized" cars from Chevrolet, Pontiac, Oldsmobile, and Buick in 1964 was a response to Ford Motor Company's 1962 Ford Fairlane and Mercury Meteor models. Pontiac, continuing to build its performance image, cut out a different niche—the muscle car—when it installed a large V-8 into its mid-sized car and called it the "GTO," shown here, a name for an Italian racing car class. Soon others were copying the idea. (N.)

GM continued its policy of offering major technological developments when it introduced the new V-8-powered front-wheel-drive Oldsmobile Toronado, shown in this ad, for 1966. The companion car from Cadillac was the front-drive Eldorado. Both represented the first high-volume, mass-production, front-drive car built in America, although the famous—and short-lived—Cord automobiles of the 1930s also featured front-drive. (OP.)

This 1967 model was Chevrolet's first Camaro. The Pontiac Firebird was its "stablemate." Both cars again were rushed out by GM in response to the highly successful introduction of Ford's Mustang "pony car" in mid-1964. While GM was pouring its resources into engineering new technical developments, Ford was putting its energy into "end run" market segmentation to thwart the stair-step system and compete with GM for customers. (N.)

The 50-story New York General Motors building, completed in 1968, was one of Manhattan's most valuable pieces of real estate, fronting on Fifth Avenue and anchoring the southeast corner of Central Park. Its 1,800,000 square feet of floor space represented more than 41 acres. Here sat GM's chairman of the board and the treasurer's office, close to Wall Street and the banks. (GA.)

Frederick G. Donner (1902–1987), left, was GM chairman from 1958 to 1967. Like his predecessors Alfred P. Sloan Jr. and Albert Bradley, he lived in New York, not Detroit. His entire 41-year GM career was spent in the treasurer's office. Thus, the positions of the GM chair and chief executive officer were widely separated from that of the president and chief operating officer, located in Detroit. Edward N. Cole (1909–1977), right, was the 14th president of General Motors from 1967–1974. An enthusiastic executive, Cole worked on the design of GM's first overhead-valve V-8, then "fathered" the '55 Chevy V-8 and the Corvair. A popular "engineer's engineer," he was the first GM president who seemed at ease with the press. (GA.)

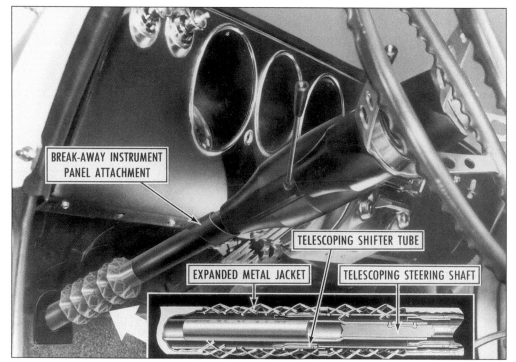

BREAK-AWAY INSTRUMENT PANEL ATTACHMENT

TELESCOPING SHIFTER TUBE

EXPANDED METAL JACKET

TELESCOPING STEERING SHAFT

A turning point came for GM and the U.S. auto industry in 1967. For the first time, vehicles came under federal regulations for safety and California rules for tailpipe emissions. GM responded with an important safety feature on all domestic 1967 GM passenger cars—the energy-absorbing steering column system shown here on a 1967 Chevrolet Camaro. The GM steering column compressed several inches in a front-end collision to protect the driver. The inset showed important parts of the safety feature. Other vehicle makers adopted the GM design. (GA.)

The year 1969 marked a curious irony in GM's overseas operations, if only for a moment in time. Opel exports for sale by Buick dealers in the United States, such as this sporty Opel GT, reached a record 93,500, exceeding the total of 84,000 for all GM exports of North American-type cars and trucks. GM foreign sales in 1969 included 802,000 from Opel, 501,000 from Canada, 286,000 from Vauxhall, 174,000 from Australia, 52,000 from Brazil, 29,000 from Argentina, 28,000 from South Africa, and 27,000 from Mexico. In contrast, GM's U.S. car divisions racked up monumentally greater sales that year: 2 million Chevrolets, 775,000 Pontiacs, 714,000 Buicks, 668,000 Oldsmobiles, and 266,000 Cadillacs. (N.)

Nine

THE WORLD COMES TO DETROIT

The mobility system for this Lunar Rover, with which Apollo 15 astronauts David R. Scott and James B. Irvin explored the moon's surface in 1971, was supplied by GM's Delco Electronics Division. This included special wire-mesh wheels, four-wheel electric drives, suspension, steering, brakes, drive-control electronics, and hand-controller. Delco also played a key role in guiding the astronauts to the moon and back safely. While GM was helping the U.S. go to the moon, its domestic market was about to be overwhelmed by foreign elements beyond its control. In the fall of 1973, the Arab Oil Embargo resulted in doubled energy costs and fear of limited fuel availability, turning the automobile market upside down in a matter of months. The American auto industry in particular was hard hit, with total car and truck sales dropping from 14.3 million in 1973 to 10.4 in 1975. The long-term result was significant growth of small imported cars in the U.S. market and ultimately, the development of smaller and more fuel-efficient cars by domestic manufacturers.

A very popular model for Chevrolet in the 1970s was this mid-sized hardtop coupe, the two-door Monte Carlo, introduced in the first year of the decade. GM dominated the market for two-door hardtops, beginning when the style was first unveiled in 1949. The sporty but roomy two-door body especially appealed to young adults, male and female. Their alternative choices in the GM family were pony cars like Camaro and Firebird. The larger coupes like the Buick Riviera and Olds Toronado appealed to an older crowd. (N.)

For its second-round counter to imports, Chevrolet introduced the subcompact Vega for its 1971 model line-up. The Vega featured a four-cylinder aluminum-block engine, which unfortunately was plagued with mechanical problems. Moreover, the Chevy Vega and rival Ford Pinto failed to capture the public's desire. Both were essentially cheaply finished economy cars lacking the full functionality and high-quality of low-cost Japanese cars beginning to penetrate the American market. However, their traditional arch-rival in the subcompact field, the VW Beetle, began to fade due to higher German costs and difficulty in meeting U.S. safety and emission regulations. (N.)

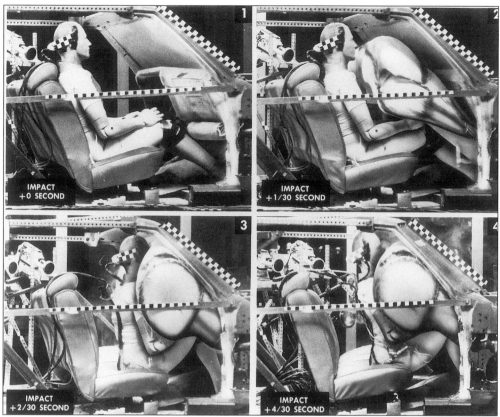

The operation of GM's Safety Air Cushion was revealed in this 1970 series of test pictures from Fisher Body Division, which developed GM's system. Taken a moment before the lab crash, Picture 1 shows the rolled-up bag stored beneath the instrument panel. The collision triggered a sensor, releasing compressed air into the bag (2). The forward momentum of the dummy, representing an unbelted car occupant, carried it into the bag instead of the windshield (3). Finally, the dummy's weight speeded deflation of the porous bag (4). GM offered such systems for sale below cost for three model years beginning with 1974 models. While it had manufacturing capacity for 100,000 a year, GM sold only 10,000 air bags during the time they were offered. (GW.)

Extending California control of pollutants nationwide, Congress mandated formation by 1970 of the Environmental Protection Agency. GM's major contribution to the environment in the early 1970s was the development of the catalytic converter to reduce auto exhaust pollutants, which has been installed on GM domestic vehicles since 1975. The AC Spark Plug Division plant in Milwaukee, Wisconsin, was GM's manufacturing source for the device, shown here, which fitted into the exhaust system between the engine and the muffler. Once again, a GM development was adopted by competitors worldwide. (GW.)

The 4,000-acre General Motors Proving Ground at Milford, Michigan, the industry's most comprehensive test facility, was pictured here as it marked its 50th year of operation in 1974, when it had 2,500 employees. The inset showed the original garage and shops in 1924 when the facility was one-quarter the present size. GM's Desert Proving Ground near Mesa, Arizona, totaled some 4,600 acres, and other U.S. special road and laboratory facilities managed by GM Engineering Staff were situated at Pike's Peak and Denver, Colorado, and Van Nuys, California. (GA.)

Exhaust emission regulations required auto companies to certify that control systems would function as designed for a minimum of 50,000 miles over a prescribed course. The volume and cost of running full-scale road tests for every vehicle powertrain combination overwhelmed auto industry proving grounds. All turned to laboratory dynamometer tests to accomplish as much as possible of the repetitive prove-out routines. Engine test cells with computerized instrumentation, such as this one at the GM Research Laboratories, provided on-line collection and processing of test data. (GW.)

This was GM's headquarters from 1922 to 1998, the General Motors Building on West Grand Boulevard in Detroit. It was here that the world's largest industrial corporation was governed by management consensus via the corporation's committee structure, supported by various staffs. The operating divisions had long been largely autonomous, in many cases managing their own staff, engineering, manufacturing, and sales activities. (GA.)

For 1976, GM took another whack at trying to compete with imported economy cars by introducing this Opel-based, U.S.-produced Chevrolet Chevette. Weighing less than 2,000 pounds and at least 17 inches shorter than any previous Chevrolet, the Chevette featured a 1.6-liter (96 cubic-inch) Four, the smallest in GM's domestic history. It was fittingly introduced in Washington, D.C., as one of the U.S. auto industry's first answers to foreign-import small cars. For a while, it was a bestseller, until faced with more space-efficient front-wheel-drive subcompacts from competitors. (GW.)

Cadillac built this Eldorado convertible on April 21, 1976, at the time, the "last convertible" produced by the American auto industry, which was once composed almost entirely of open cars. A popular novel and television mini-series were even inspired around the theme. With air conditioning and worries about safety, the public's demand for the body style had dropped to practically nothing—until convertibles were no longer available. GM resumed convertible production with the 1982 Buick Riviera. (CH.)

Anticipating federal regulation of fuel economy even before the Corporate Average Fuel Economy (CAFE) legislation of 1976, GM began down-sizing its larger cars with the 1977 model year. The result was smaller, lighter and more fuel-efficient full-sized cars like this '79 Cadillac Sedan de Ville. (CH.)

For 1978, GM mid-size cars were redesigned to increase mileage. This chart showed how the new Pontiac LeMans lost weight—which translated into fuel economy gains—but increased interior dimensions versus the 1977 model. Some thought the new mid-sized models were boxy and not as attractive as the ones they replaced, but it was an era of function over form. (GA.)

1977-78 GRAND LEMANS FOUR—DOOR SEDAN COMPARISONS

Grand LeMans

EXTERIOR	1978	1977	1977-78 CHANGE
Length	198.5"	212.0"	− 13.5"
Width	72.4"	77.4"	− 5.0"
Wheelbase	108.1"	116.0"	− 7.9"
Weight	3167 lbs.	3856 lbs.	−689 lbs.
INTERIOR			
Front Head Room	38.7"	37.9"	+ .80"
Rear Head Room	37.7"	37.2"	+ .50"
Front Leg Room	42.8"	42.5"	+ .30"
Rear Leg Room	38.0"	37.0"	+ 1.0"
Rear Knee Clearance	1.7"	− 1.4"	+ 3.1"
LUGGAGE CAPACITY	16.4 Cu. Ft.	15.1 Cu. Ft.	+ 1.3 Cu. Ft.

Another mid-sized car made lighter and more fuel efficient was this 1978 Oldsmobile Cutlass Supreme. From the late 1970s into the mid-1980s, the Cutlass coupe was usually the largest selling car model in America and helped Oldsmobile sales top the one million mark in 1977, 1978, 1979, 1984, 1985, and 1986. (GA.)

In 1978, with this Regency 98, Oldsmobile pioneered passenger-car diesels among U.S. automakers. By 1983, many GM car lines offered either V-6 or V-8 diesels. Unfortunately, few Americans car buyers were willing to suffer noisy, sluggish performance and hard-to-find fuel in exchange for the diesel's greater economy of operation. Deserved or not, diesels developed a sour reputation with the U.S. public, whether installed by GM or Volkswagen. (GW.)

This 1980 Cadillac Seville was GM's last production car styled under the direction of William L. "Bill" Mitchell, architect of the '38 Cadillac Sixty Special (page 52) and the man who succeeded Harley Earl as styling vice president in 1958. This Seville's style married a highly acclaimed "London look" with the "sheer" treatments introduced on the previous 1976 Seville and the 1977 "down-sized" GM cars. Although controversial at the time, today many collectors consider it a modern classic. (CH.)

Ten

REORGANIZING FOR
WORLD COMPETITION

The decade of the 1970s closed with another external event beyond any corporate anticipation or control, the extremist Iranian Revolution, again threatening fuel availability and, in just weeks, upsetting the domestic auto market. The 1980s thus started dourly for GM and other western-world producers, plagued by inflation, a need for massive reinvestment in more economical vehicles, and a strong challenge from Japanese companies. General Motors Corporation suffered its first annual loss since 1921, $763 million in 1980, and GM's international operations lost money in every year from 1980 through 1986. The official caption for this photograph taken of new and old GM management teams read: "Exchanging congratulations immediately following announcement on September 9, 1980, of forthcoming changes in GM leadership are (l to r) Roger B. Smith, named chairman, F. James McDonald, president, Howard H. Kehrl, vice chairman, Thomas A. Murphy, retiring chairman and Elliott M. Estes, retiring president." (GA.)

In its new models of the 1980s, GM embraced front-wheel-drive and transverse-mounted engines—heretofore incorporated only on small foreign cars—for GM cars of all sizes. They started with a new family of compact cars, called the "X-cars" in development, as illustrated by this 1980 Chevrolet Citation. Companion cars of the same basic design were the Pontiac Phoenix, Oldsmobile Omega, and Buick Skylark. They offered another step in improved gas mileage and, despite boxy styling, initially had strong sales. (N.)

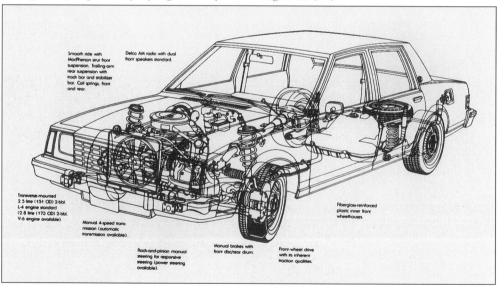

This "cutaway" or "phantom" view of the 1980 Buick Skylark illustrates the radical new engine-transmission layout of GM's "X cars," featuring either a four-cylinder 90-horsepower engine or an optional 115-horsepower V-6. Both coupes and sedans were mounted on a 105-inch wheelbase, seated five passengers, and carried 14.3 cubic feet of cargo. The Skylark was 19 inches shorter, 5 inches narrower, and some 750 pounds lighter than its 1979 predecessor. (GA.)

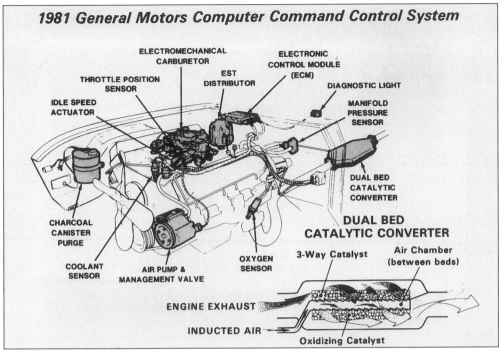

1981 General Motors Computer Command Control System

ELECTROMECHANICAL CARBURETOR

ELECTRONIC CONTROL MODULE (ECM)

THROTTLE POSITION SENSOR

EST DISTRIBUTOR

DIAGNOSTIC LIGHT

IDLE SPEED ACTUATOR

MANIFOLD PRESSURE SENSOR

CHARCOAL CANISTER PURGE

DUAL BED CATALYTIC CONVERTER

COOLANT SENSOR

AIR PUMP & MANAGEMENT VALVE

OXYGEN SENSOR

DUAL BED CATALYTIC CONVERTER

3-Way Catalyst

Air Chamber (between beds)

ENGINE EXHAUST

INDUCTED AIR

Oxidizing Catalyst

The development of automotive electronic components that could be produced reliably in mass production helped GM and others meet increasingly stringent fuel economy and emission controls. This is a diagram of GM's Computer Command Control (CCC) exhaust emission system, used in this or subsequent forms on GM vehicles since 1981. The CCC system regulated air/fuel mixture and controlled the Air Injection Reactor pump output so that the catalytic converter operated at optimum efficiency. The major CCC system functions included control of engine spark advance, speed, and transmission torque converter clutch, which helped to improve fuel economy. (GW.)

GM introduced its third major group of front-wheel-drive cars and its first front-drive mid-sized cars with 1982 models of the Buick Century, Chevrolet Celebrity, Pontiac 6000 (shown here in a 1983 model), and Oldsmobile Cutlass Ciera. With this entry, there were now eight different Chevrolet passenger car models produced: the full-sized Chevrolet, the mid-sized rear-drive Monte Carlo, the mid-sized front-drive Celebrity, the compact Citation, the subcompact Cavalier and Chevettes, and the sporty Camaro and Corvette. The B-O-P Divisions offered similar overlapping ranges. Sloan's philosophy of distinct prices and model attributes separating the brands now was ancient history. (PH.)

In an unusual move heralding a new era in labor relations, in March 1982, GM and the UAW—without a strike threat—signed new labor agreements seven months before the expiration of the old contract. The new contract emphasized improvements in competitiveness, quality of work life, and job security provisions. At the settlement, sitting at left, was Owen Bieber, the UAW vice president who succeeded Douglas Fraser (center) as UAW president in 1983, and—significantly—Roger B. Smith, the new GM chairman. It had been traditional for GM chairmen to live and manage from New York before Tom Murphy, Smith's predecessor, moved to Detroit. Now Smith was breaking another shibboleth by becoming involved face-to-face in labor negotiations, if only for the wind-up. (GA.)

To modernize and become more production-efficient in the 1980s, GM embarked on a massive robotics program. "Flexible automation," exemplified by these robot welders, was applied on an ever-increasing scale to increase productivity and improve product quality as part of a $40-billion spending program for new products, plants, and manufacturing and assembly processes. However, looked at some years afterward, it appears that robots and other automation GM adopted failed to provide the level of benefits expected.

GM broke new ground for 1982 by introducing the first domestically made compact pickup trucks, the Chevrolet S-10 and the GMC S-15, shown here. Previously, Chevrolet had contracted with GM's Japanese affiliate, Isuzu, for the Chevy Luv pickup. A 1.9-liter (120-cubic-inch) L-4 engine was standard with a V-6 optional in GM's new small trucks. Rival Ford was a year behind. (GW.)

The following year, 1983, GM again "blazed" new ground with this compact Chevy Blazer four-wheel-drive sports utility vehicle based on the S-10. The new Blazer was 15 inches shorter and 15 inches narrower than the conventional full-sized Blazer built on the Chevy CK truck chassis. The companion new model from the GMC Truck and Coach Division was the GMC Jimmy. Again Ford trailed with its Bronco II. (GW.)

This GMC 8000 series diesel-powered Brigadier for 1982 was close to the last of a line of heavy and extra-heavy trucks GMC had been offering since the earliest days of the corporation. Now GM's largest-scale disinvestment in the 1980s involved the heavy truck and bus businesses. Withdrawal from the heavy truck business came in several steps. First, in 1981, Bedford operations were merged with those of GM's Chevrolet and GMC North American heavy truck operations, which were split from the fast-growing light truck business. Overseas, GM joined with Japanese partner Isuzu to participate in the heavy truck business. In North America, GM formed a joint venture with Volvo for the heavy truck business, the Volvo GM Heavy Truck Corporation, with operational responsibility handed over to Volvo. And, GM sold a majority of its Detroit Diesel engine business to the Penske Group. (N.)

The Long Beach (California) Public Transportation Co. was the nation's first transit system to operate this new RTS (Rapid Transit Series) bus from GMC in 1983. It was one of the last GMC bus designs before the business was sold to Greyhound. (GA.)

GM's first complete vehicle instrument clusters were built by its AC Spark Plug Division in Flint in 1928. Contrast the earlier generation gauges, top, with a 1984 Chevrolet Corvette liquid-crystal-display electronic instrument cluster, bottom. The pioneering LCD cluster, also manufactured by AC, displayed speed, fuel, and r.p.m., with the speedometer and tachometer sections in both digital (numeric) and analog (curvilinear) bar-graph form. The electronic cluster also included a "driver information center." (GA.)

With government-mandated fuel economy standards ever increasing in stringency, the effect of automobile body aerodynamics became an important consideration in design. This shows a technician/operator at the console of the GM Tech Center wind tunnel, monitoring an aerodynamic test of the a 1984 Corvette. (GW.)

In 1983, GM's 75th anniversary year, the latest state-of-the-art in locomotive power was this high-adhesion SD50, produced by Electro-Motive Division. GM stated that it was the most fuel-efficient locomotive in America. Incorporating a new wheel-control system, the SD50 used radar and solid-state integrated circuit technology to raise the attainable adhesion level by one-third. (GW.)

Continuing its policy of introducing radical new mass-production product concepts to the American market, in1984 GM brought out this cute two-passenger mid-engined Pontiac Fiero. Dealers hailed it for bringing new traffic into their showrooms after a period of otherwise rather uninspiring cars. Automobile writers loved it because of its adventuresome layout and plastic body panels. First-year sales exceeded 100,000 units. It especially appealed to the rapidly rising market segment of single young women. But according to latter-day critics, once again a new product failed to achieve GM's cost and quality aims, and the Fiero was dropped from the market in 1988. (PH.)

This Oldsmobile advertisement for a 1985 front-wheel-drive '98 Regency illustrated the final step in GM's switch to front-wheel-drive cars. After this, the remaining rear-drive models were phased out over a ten-year period. The biggest criticism of the large-body front-drivers was that their functional but boxy styling failed to hold up to GM's traditional leadership role in the beauty department. Traditional GM large-car customers had come to expect the feel of their big V-8s and rear-drive luxury and resisted the new front-drive V-6 models.

In the celebration of its 75th birthday in 1983, GM used this Fisher Body Plant in Livonia, Michigan, as a prime example of its new plant architecture. But the days of the Fisher Body Division, autonomous since the 1920s, were nearly over. GM's top officials realized that the corporation had grown into a very unwieldy, inefficient structure with its many supplier divisions and assembly operations under different management, most dating from their acquisition in the Durant days. To correct this, manufacturing was reorganized, eliminating Fisher and its separate-management Siamese-twin attachment to assembly plants. The historical vehicle divisions likewise were consolidated into Chevrolet-Pontiac-Canada and Buick-Oldsmobile-Cadillac in 1984, losing their separate engineering and assembly operations. (GA.)

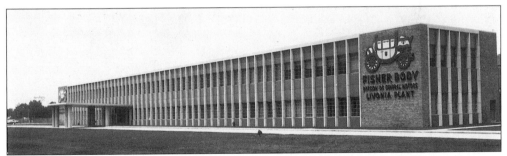

Roger B. Smith (1925–) served as the tenth chairman of GM, 1981–1990. Like previous chairmen, he had risen in the Finance Staff in New York. However, he followed the precedent of his immediate predecessor, Tom Murphy, electing to function as chairman from Detroit. Further, he took an active role in operating matters, unprecedented since the early Sloan days, and he eagerly pushed programs and products he felt the times called for. As such, he was GM's first truly "public" chairman. Initially he was lionized by the media because of GM's more-efficient-seeming, advanced-appearing designs and policies. But as GM's hold on the American market continued to slide, critics spared no words. If wrong things were not done for the right reasons in his regime, then the apparently right things too often did not work out as expected. (GA.)

GM announced on February 14, 1983, that it was forming a joint venture—New United Motor Manufacturing Inc., or NUMMI—with Japan's Toyota Motor Corp. to produce a small Chevrolet in this Fremont, California plant previously operated by GM. The agreement gave GM an opportunity to learn about efficient Japanese production methods and became an incubator for GM future top management. The plant began producing a Toyota-derived sub-compact Chevrolet Nova in mid-1985 and the Toyota Corolla in 1986. Two years later, the plant switched to a new Corolla and its version for GM, the Geo Prizm. (GA.)

Pictured on this page are GM's three principal overseas-produced cars in its 75th anniversary year. At the top is a German Opel Kadett, boasting a 1.8-liter engine and front-wheel drive. In the center is a British-built, right-hand-drive 90-horsepower Vauxhall Cavalier. GM consolidated its Opel and Vauxhall car designs at Opel following a 1978 reorganization of overseas operations. The first new "common car" of the strategy was the front-wheel-drive Opel Ascona/Vauxhall Cavalier introduced for the European medium segment in 1981. When GM's new Zaragoza, Spain plant started up late in 1982, its Opel Corsa/Vauxhall Nova was hailed as "the smallest and most fuel-efficient gasoline-powered car ever offered by General Motors." Front-wheel-drive Holden Camira and Brazilian Chevrolet Monza models were also introduced in 1982. At the bottom is a unibody Holden Commodore, also right-hand-drive, GM's first internationally-styled car designed for Australia. (GW.)

Many Detroit observers felt GM abdicated its long-time styling leadership to Ford and its rounded "jelly bean" designs in the 1980s. Here, clay modelers at GM Design Staff worked inside a studio giving three dimensions to a future car concept. Clay modeling was the step that came after sketched renderings (page 74) and preliminary management approvals in the design process. From such a full-sized clay model, market research could be conducted and production dies scanned by computers into final manufacturing form. (GW.)

The 1984 GM Harrison Radiator Division aluminum radiator, left, illustrated a remarkable transition in design and materials in cars and cooling systems, compared to the 1926 copper Chevrolet radiator at right. The newer aluminum design featured plastic tanks and integral transmission oil cooler. Compared to the 1926 radiator, it was 24 pounds lighter (weighing only 8 pounds) and capable of transferring seven times more heat under identical conditions. The change in car design was reflected in the shapes—low and wide versus high and narrow. (GA.)

The auto industry's first robot painting system, shown here, went into operation in 1983 at GM's Doraville, Georgia assembly plant. It was designed to switch from body style to body style, and from color to color, automatically and easily. The photo shows the robot "door operator" that opened and closed car doors to allow painting of the interior. According to industry reports, such robots did not always obey their instructions, disrupting production and cramping hoped-for productivity advances. (GW.)

Lines of huge metal-stamping presses like this were installed in GM's metal fabricating plants where components such as doors, roofs, underbodies, and hundreds of other large and small parts were manufactured from coils of steel. In the 1990s, GM ran into difficult labor-relations problems at certain such plants as employees resisted modernization efforts that cost jobs. Independent manufacturing analysts rated GM's metal-stamping plants the most inefficient in the domestic auto industry. (GW.)

As GM sought different strategies to cope with the continued growth of foreign, especially Japanese, competition in the American market, one solution they conceived was the creation from scratch of "a new kind of car company." This was accomplished with the development of the Saturn project, embodying a wholly new design not sharing parts with other GM cars, a new plant, a new customer-oriented dealer organization, and a new order of working relationships throughout, akin to Japanese companies. This aerial showed the Saturn Car Company complex in Spring Hill, Tennessee, launched in 1990. (S.)

Shown here are Saturn's second-generation 1999 models, including the four-door sedan, the wagon, and the coupe. Saturn quickly established very high owner-satisfaction rankings and owner loyalty. The flaw in the strategy was that initially there was no provision for a "step-up" model from the basic Saturn four-cylinder compact car, as Sloan would have required. At the end of 1999, a larger Saturn was on the way, built at another GM plant in Delaware and sharing major design elements with other GM cars. (S.)

Following a management rout triggered by outside directors who were concerned with GM's plummeting financial performance in North America, John F. "Jack" Smith Jr. (1938–), at right, was named president and chief executive officer in 1992. The new non-executive chairman of the board was John G. Smale, an outside director since 1982 and former chairman of Procter & Gamble. GM's board had become much smaller, with outside directors far outnumbering GM executives. Smith was a financial executive who was part of the NUMMI team in 1983 and subsequently headed GM of Canada, GM of Europe, and finally, as vice chairman in 1990, GM's International Operations, which he returned to high profitability and dominance over Ford. (GW.)

While GM sold off several large businesses—road-building equipment, heavy trucks, and buses—in the 1980s, it also made significant acquisitions: Electronic Data Systems (EDS) in 1984 and Hughes Aircraft in 1985. On the global front, GM purchased 50 percent of Saab Automobile AB of Sweden in 1989. This is a 1994 Saab 900 convertible, one of the Swedish automaker's most popular models, especially in the North American market. (N.)

When the Berlin Wall in Germany came down, GM was one of the first companies to cross over into the East, establishing this new state-of-the-art Opel plant at Eisenach. In 1996, it employed around 1,200 men and women working in two shifts. The facility covered an area of approximately 300,000 square meters. (O.)

This Opel Corsa was pictured at an ancient castle in the former East Germany. With the start of production of the three-door model variant at Eisenach, the Corsa was being manufactured for the first time outside Zaragoza in Spain. In 1995, the Eisenach plant was honored for being the most efficient auto assembler in Europe. (O.)

A 1905 Model C Buick and a 1993 Park Avenue Ultra were admired here by Buick chief engineer Tony Derhake, left, and general manager Ed Mertz at Buick headquarters, then in Flint, during Buick's 90th anniversary celebration in 1993. The Model C shown here was believed to be the fourth-oldest Buick in existence and the first ever sold in California. Buick built 729 Model Cs in 1905 and 58 in 1906. The oldest known surviving Buicks were 14 Model Cs. (BH.)

In this 1995 advertisement, Oldsmobile promoted its all-new Aurora, a unique vehicle not sharing major components with any other GM cars. Aurora was aimed at upscale buyers of imported luxury sedans, those who presumably would never consider "their father's Oldsmobile," so Oldsmobile identity was played down. Blatant price advertising for luxury cars was highly unusual, but new brand-merchandising strategists felt the $32,000 price would be a bargain for target buyers. (OP.)

This 1996 Chevrolet Impala was the last of Chevy's rear-wheel drive cars. The name harked back to an earlier era; Impala was first used on the top-of-the-line 1958 Chevrolet but began to be supplanted by Caprice in 1965. The end of rear-wheel-drive Chevys also "sounded taps" for conventional Chevrolet police cars and taxis, leaving the field open exclusively to Ford. (CP.)

This 1996 Buick Roadmaster Limited Estate Wagon was the last full-sized rear-wheel-drive station wagon offered in America by any automaker. In the 1950s and 1960s, such models were popular as family cars before the era of minivans and SUVs. The wagon shared its chassis with the Chevrolet Impala, above. (BP.)

This was the instrument panel of the 1997 Opel Sintra minivan, a family vehicle built in GM's Doraville, Georgia assembly plant along with companion vehicles carrying Vauxhall, Chevrolet, Pontiac, and Oldsmobile nameplates. It offers an interesting contrast to earlier instrument panels pictured elsewhere in this book. (O.)

Here is the right-hand-drive Vauxhall version of the Sintra, designed for the British market. This "universal" vehicle was built with a 3.4-liter V-6 for the Chevrolet Venture, Pontiac Trans Sport, and Oldsmobile Silhouette North American vehicles. A British-built 3.0-liter V-6 and a new Opel 2.2-liter 16-valve Four were built for Europe. The Vauxhall and Opel versions represented the first time cars with those nameplates were produced in North America, specifically designed to augment U.S. exports. European buyers, however, did not accept the vans, and after 1999, they were to be replaced by a smaller Opel design. The American versions were considered highly successful, if late to the marketplace. (O.)

The Omega was Opel's top-of-the-line model in Europe, produced with variations as a Vauxhall for Britain and a Holden in Australia. This is a '94 Omega station wagon. In the last year of the 1980s, Opel factory sales from Germany of 1,332,792 exceeded, for the first time, those of Chevrolet, which came in at 1,194,975. The Opel Kadett was the company's largest selling car worldwide. (N.)

The Opel Omega entered the U.S. market in 1996 as the Cadillac Catera. Pictured is a 1998 model. This was an outstanding example of GM's successful "common car" strategy across several national borders and cultures. The rear-wheel-drive Catera was intended by Cadillac to be competitive with other imported luxury sedans in the North American market. (C.)

Under Jack Smith, GM formed a new president's council that replaced, in many respects, the Sloan committee system. Shown here, in a portrait for the 1997 GM Annual Report, are the following members, from left to right; Louis R. Hughes, G. Richard Wagoner Jr., J.T. Battenberg III, Smith, J. Michael Losh, and Harry J. Pearce. At the time, Smith was chairman and chief executive officer, Pearce was vice chairman, and the others, executive vice presidents. (GA.)

Here's something you won't mind raking in this season.

Buick's *Fall Collection* E V E N T

'98 Century

'98 Regal

'98 Park Avenue Ultra

'98 Riviera

'98 LeSabre

As shown in this advertisement for the Buick line at the end of the 1998 model year, Buick had managed to maintain its identity through common design themes—the traditional "waterfall" grille on all except the Regal (second from left) and an oval-shaped back panel. Unlike some contemporary GM cars, there was no mystery as to the make of a Buick. The Riviera luxury coupe (second from right), first introduced for 1963, was dropped at the end of 1998 as GM moved to reduce its number of vehicle platforms. (M.)

After Oldsmobile discontinued the installation of V-8 engines, its old nomenclature—dating back to the "Rocket" V-8 engine in 1949—no longer made sense. For example, a rocket had long been the brand's symbol. Likewise, model designations such as "88" and "98" originally indicated that the cars were powered by eight-cylinder engines. Thus Olds came up with a new symbol in the 1990s, this oval-shaped, stylized "O" shown as a dealership sign, and also introduced new models with new names no longer associated with the past. (OP.)

123

In response to the threats of California environmentalists to require all new cars to have "zero emissions," GM spent millions to develop this EV-1 battery-electric vehicle. It was offered for lease through Saturn dealers in California and the Phoenix, Arizona area. There were few takers, but GM had demonstrated its willingness to offer such new technology and the futility of regulators trying to force unwanted products on the public. The objection to electric vehicles in 1999 was the same as it had been a century earlier—limited range. (N.)

As shown on this 1999 Pontiac Grand Am, Pontiac designers returned to a version of the 1936–1956 "silver streak" theme as they sought to make their cars stand out from the crowd. Most Pontiac models incorporate the three-dimensional horizontal ribbing in their front and side design. Even more than Buick, you can easily distinguish a Pontiac. (PP.)

This is the 1999 Chevrolet Prism, the GM version of the Toyota Corolla, jointly produced together at the NUMMI plant in California, and one of three sub-compacts of fundamentally Japanese design successfully sold by Chevrolet. The others are the Suzuki-designed Metro and Tracker SUV made by the GM-Suzuki joint venture in Canada called CAMI. (CP.)

For mid-1998, GM introduced the long-awaited newest version of its standard pickup trucks, the '99-model Chevrolet Silverado, shown here, and the GMC Sierra. Such full-sized trucks had become the largest selling vehicles in the world and, along with their enclosed sports-utility versions, among the most profitable for a manufacturer. The launch was marred by a long strike by UAW employees in Flint who were unwilling to adopt competitive production practices. (CP.)

Chevrolet returned for the 2000 model year to one of its best-known model names, Impala, for its new six-passenger $19,265 family sedan, shown here. The new Impala was a front-drive model with round taillamps like the original '58 model. The new car was 9 inches shorter and 4 inches narrower than the original with a choice of two V-6 engines, a 180-horsepower 3.4-liter and a 205-horsepower 3.8-liter, versus a 145-horsepower Six and V-8s of 185 to 315 horsepower in 1958. The weight is almost the same, but the 2000 model carried a much higher level of standard equipment, such as air conditioning. (CP.)

This is the latest version of the flagship of GM's worldwide vehicle output, the model 2000 Cadillac Deville, entering the 97th year of the brand's production. The top-of-the-line 2000 Cadillac was down-sized from previous models. While riding on a longer 115.4-inch wheelbase, at 207 inches long the car is 2 inches shorter than the 1999 Deville and also 2 inches narrower, though still retaining the same interior space. Compared to the 1958 Sedan deVille in GM's 50th anniversary year, the 2000 is 10 inches shorter and about 900 pounds lighter. The new Cadillac introduced a remarkable safety innovation, a night-vision option using infrared technology to help drivers see beyond their headlight illumination after dark. (C.)

In 1996, General Motors bought the Renaissance Center, erected by Henry Ford II on Detroit's waterfront during the 1970s, and proceeded to consolidate its principal executive offices there from the older GM Building in Detroit's New Center area, as well as from Flint, Lansing, Pontiac, and Warren. A major GM concern had become its shrinking share of the U.S. auto market, down to 30 percent from more than 60 at its peak. (D.)

The Buick Cielo concept car, shown here, may or may not be in GM's future. The fully operational "dream" four-door convertible with retracting "hard" top panels and rear window was unveiled at the 1999 North American International Automobile Show in Detroit to test public reaction and attract attention to Buicks on sale at the time. The car's traditional Buick "waterfall" grille design, not seen in this rear view, maintained the brand identity. (BP.)

ACKNOWLEDGMENTS

I am indebted to many people for their assistance in producing this book, but being human, I may forget some, for which I hope no feelings will be hurt.

First, there were three people who assisted me in becoming familiar with the history of General Motors: David Smith of Ward's Communications, who assigned me to research and write a history of General Motors' overseas operations for a special project yet to be published; Jack Harned, then with the GM Public Relations Staff and since retired; and Sue Petre, GM's head business librarian.

Second, there are those who assisted directly in this "Picture History of General Motors," beginning with GM's new vice president-communications, Steven J. Harris; Larry Gustin of Buick Public Relations, a published automotive historian himself; Laura Mancini and Kim Schroeder of GM's Media Archives; Jim Mattison of Pontiac Historic Services; Gary Wallace of Cadillac Historic Services; Helen Earley of the Olds Historic Center; Mark Patrick, director of the National Automotive History Collection at the Detroit Public Library; Tom Featherstone of the Reuther Library at Wayne State University; friends Charles K. Hyde and Douglas N. Williams who provided encouragement; and John Kelvin, who saved me much typing by letting me use his company's scanner.

Third, my wife, Karen, exercised infinite patience while I buried myself in the project the better part of a year.